D1361829

Hidden
Brilliance

UNLOCKING THE
INTELLIGENCE OF AUTISM

Hidden Brilliance

Lynn Kern Koegel, PhD,
and Claire LaZebnik

HARPER WAVE
An Imprint of HarperCollins*Publishers*

HIDDEN BRILLIANCE. Copyright © 2023 by Lynn Kern Koegel and Claire LaZebnik. All rights reserved. Printed in the United States of America. No part of this book may be used or reproduced in any manner whatsoever without written permission except in the case of brief quotations embodied in critical articles and reviews. For information, address HarperCollins Publishers, 195 Broadway, New York, NY 10007.

HarperCollins books may be purchased for educational, business, or sales promotional use. For information, please email the Special Markets Department at SPsales@harpercollins.com.

FIRST EDITION

Design by Elina Cohen
Title page art courtesy of Shutterstock / lyricsai

Library of Congress Cataloging-in-Publication Data has been applied for.

ISBN 978-0-06-322537-4

23 24 25 26 27 LBC 5 4 3 2 1

HB 02.01.2023 0910

DEDICATED TO OUR FAMILIES, WHOSE SUPPORT IS UNFLAGGING AND UNCONDITIONAL, WITH EXTRA GRATITUDE TO OUR NEURODIVERSE RELATIVES AND FRIENDS, WHOSE STORIES AND BRILLIANCE LIGHT UP OUR LIVES AND THE PAGES OF THIS BOOK.

Contents

Preface

We started writing books together about autism more than twenty years ago, and Lynn has been part of the autism world for a couple of decades longer than that. We've both seen a *lot* of autism-related trends, treatments, attitudes, and assumptions come and go, and it's always a relief to see outdated and misguided ideas disappear from the conversation.

Overall, the changes in the last twenty years or so have been positive. Although the research is still woefully inadequate, there's more than there used to be to help guide us toward better ways to help individuals on the autism spectrum reach their full potential. Additionally, the way we think and talk about autism has changed, and there's more awareness about the importance and benefits of diversity and tolerance in our communities. We're thrilled that so many people are willing to open their hearts and minds to those who may look, talk, worship, and/or love differently than they do. And we're saddened and frustrated by those who aren't willing to take that leap.

There are many wonderful and brilliant people with autism, who are pushing for acceptance on their own terms, and who, justifiably and rightfully, have no desire to be forced to conform to other people's expectations or rules. We heartily support that. No one should have to change who they are to make other people more comfortable.

We also feel that connection to others and being part of a community is a vital, meaningful part of life, and that everyone should have the opportunity to know these joys. Sometimes this involves learning something new. A simple metaphor might be traveling to another country for an extended stay: if you never learn the language or customs, you might feel isolated, and you won't be exposed to new ideas and activities that could be life changing. But if you make the effort to learn enough about your new home to be able to interact with the people who live there and to become part of their community, you will not only enrich your own life, but you'll enrich the society around you by sharing your own different and potentially mind-opening viewpoints with others. Learning a new language doesn't eradicate or invalidate your original, native language: it simply adds to it. Nor does learning about the customs of the people around you mean you have to conform to them, if you prefer your own (although you may discover you want to adopt some of the things you've learned about). Knowledge of other cultures simply creates a bridge between you and everyone around you, and you are all richer for it.

Connection and diversity make every society wiser, kinder, more welcoming, and just *better*. Everything in this book is to help our children, our communities, and our world find the meaningful connections that open hearts and minds.

What We're Talking About
When We Talk About Teaching Methods

An important concept throughout this book is the importance of motivation. Motivational strategies are tried-and-true teaching procedures that should be used with *all* children: they play a fundamental role in bringing out anyone's potential. We'll be discussing them in far greater detail later in the book, but for now just understand that by "motivational strategies," we're referring to engaging and delighting a child, adolescent, or adult by using their unique interests and strengths when teaching them. We all learn best when we're interested in what we're studying and having fun. Feeling bored or being threatened with punishment will never spur anyone to greater involvement by choice; being fascinated and discovering inherent rewards in every lesson will.

Our goal in writing this book is to provide everyone with the opportunity to reach their maximum potential by focusing on motivational ways of teaching, and by educating the larger community in supporting, accepting, and embracing the gifts autistic individuals offer.

A Few Quick Notes About Language

As far as we can tell, some members of the autism community prefer to be described as "autistic," and others prefer the terms "having autism," or "being on the autism spectrum," while there are those who prefer the more general "person with ASD." And so on. If there were a final consensus of the most respectful way to identify members of this community, we would absolutely stick to that, but since we find opinions vary, we've also chosen to vary the terms we use in this book. Whether that means no one will find fault with us or everyone will find fault with us remains to be seen. We imagine we'll end up somewhere in the middle.

Also, you may notice as you read through the book (and even this Foreword) that we lean heavily on the pronoun "they" as a general use pronoun, even when we're using a singular subject—something we were both taught *not* to ever do when we were kids. (We were also taught not to split an infinitive, so maybe we're just born rebels.) A strict grammarian may be frustrated by sentences like "Visit your child's classroom and get to know their teacher," and we get it. It does sound odd to older ears, but we'd rather sound odd and be inclusive of anyone and everyone, no matter how they identify, than exclude anyone. Saying "He or she or they" over and over again would get awfully cumbersome after a while, so "they" it is!

We also hope that readers will forgive us the laziness of using the term "parents," when referring to any and all guardians and/or caregivers responsible for the welfare and upbringing of a child. We understand that many who love and care for autistic children are grandparents, aunts, uncles, siblings, foster parents, etc., and we recognize that families come in all shapes and sizes. Once again, we're choosing a simple solution to keep the word count brief, and "parent" is just our shorthand for the child's caregiver, whoever that may be.

Repetition

If you read this book straight through from beginning to end, you'll gain a certain familiarity with some of our key concepts. You may even feel like we're repeating ourselves a bit. That's because a lot of what's true for supporting your child in one area will be equally valid for supporting them in another. For example: as we explained above, we believe in motivating your child to stay engaged by incorporating their favorite toys, interests, and activities into every learning opportunity. So references to "motivational procedures" crop up quite a bit in the book, and we're likely to throw in a quick reminder/explanation of what that means almost every time we mention them. If something's an important thing to note and remember in one area, it's probably going to be equally important in another, and we'd rather hammer these things home than risk being unclear.

Support for All

Over the last decade or so, it has become increasingly challenging to figure out the right tone for a book about autism that's aimed at parents of children on the spectrum. Parents and educators are often struggling with a child's interfering behaviors and communication challenges. They deserve empathy and support, but the autism advocacy movement has understandably and rightfully been working hard to combat negative stereotypes and anti-autism sentiments. It's a delicate balance to advise without giving offense. Above all, we want to help people find the connections that enrich their lives. And we definitely want to do this in a way that's enjoyable for everyone involved.

Please understand that our intention is to support every member of every family to the best of our abilities, and to encourage love, success, celebration, and triumphs. We both have close relatives on the autism spectrum and are always mindful of the work still needed to ensure good teaching, thoughtful learning environments, acceptance, and tolerance. Our goal is to identify the gifts and potential that must be nurtured, fostered, encouraged, and supported for the most successful learning and outcomes.

We hope you find this book helpful in every possible way!

Hidden
Brilliance

CHAPTER 1

Hidden Strengths

Joey can draw a character from any TV show he's seen in about three seconds. He's only five, and this totally impresses his friends. Andrew can name any movie theme song after just two notes. His peers beg the teacher to let him display his skills for the class. Arturo knows every train and airplane route in the world by heart. He loves to give advice, so family and friends consult him before they travel. Meghan and Diego have no spoken words, but she can locate tiny hidden pictures in any drawing, and he can find his favorite app on his mom's phone in mere moments. Julia has memorized all the liner notes to every song by her favorite artist. Every year the kids nominate her to be in the school talent show—and then argue about who'll get to introduce her.

All of these children are autistic . . . and also, undeniably, brilliant. Recognizing a child's exceptional abilities is crucial for developing and achieving social communication goals.

We want everyone reading this book to focus on the brilliance in the child in front of them, to delight in that child's strengths, to nurture their talents, and to brag about their triumphs. The rewards of doing this range from improving your own emotional life, to being able to encourage others to bring out the best in your child, to knowing you can support them in a far more positive and successful way than one based on ferreting out weaknesses and deficits.

Simply switching from the mind-set of focusing on the negative to finding and focusing on the positives will have enormous impacts in every area of your family's life. This book will serve as a guide to identifying the brilliance and talents of your child and using them to engage, support, and teach your child in a way that everyone will find enjoyable and successful. Determining areas of strength and incorporating them into activities will elevate your child's learning, socialization, engagement, and happiness.

Most parents feel certain that their kids are smarter than their scores and grades might indicate. Whether or not that's true is, of course, often up for debate. On the one hand, testing can be unreliable. On the other hand, we parents are a biased group. But when you're talking about children on the autism spectrum, as well as those with many other developmental differences, the odds are extremely high that their parents' suspicions *are* correct, and their kids are significantly brighter and more capable than testing, classroom performance, and traditional academic achievement are likely to show.

The intelligence and abilities of children and young adults on the autism spectrum are too often overlooked and misjudged by those who rely on evaluation methods that don't take into account neurodiverse ways of learning, communicating, and behaving. Professionals present standardized test results to parents as some kind of predictor of future success—or lack thereof—with no acknowledgment of how flawed the system is for anyone with differences. Or, in some cases, the child may have acquired the skill the test is designed to tease out, but the testing materials and/or pictures differ from what the child is familiar with, which prevents them from answering correctly, which they might have done if different, more familiar stimuli had been presented. As a result, students with differences, who are fully capable of doing interesting and meaningful schoolwork, are instead frequently given tasks and problems below their abilities.

In this book, we'll explore the reasons, both obvious and subtle, why this is true—and why it's vital that we challenge the conclusions people draw about our kids. We'll also discuss the many ways that teachers, administrators, diagnosticians, therapists, other professionals, and, most crucially, family members can discover, nurture, and utilize a child's interests, strengths, and passions, not only to make a difference each and every day, but also to improve long-term outcomes. There are numerous authenticated ways to help autistic children, adolescents, and adults embrace, enjoy, and make the most of their intelligence and understanding, leading to fulfilling experiences and outcomes. We're going to be exploring those in this book, using real-life stories of individuals with ASD who were capable of far more than the adults around them realized, and whose innate brilliance and sensitivity, once recognized and encouraged, blossomed. (A note: while the anecdotes are all true, names have been changed to protect everyone's privacy.)

Too often in the autism world, people can fall into the habit of focusing on unwanted or different behaviors. It's understandable: there's a tendency to feel like we need to "fix" weaknesses or deficits, and that idea can lead to searching them out. But, as we'll explain, strengths work as a springboard to learning and engagement, and should be where our focus lies. These positives might take a bit more effort to home in on, but they're there, and, once identified, can create an entirely different trajectory for a child.

Lynn's Personal Story: A Little History

Teddy (a pseudonym) was a beautiful but extremely fussy baby. Whether it was colic or the initial signs of autism spectrum disorder, we'll never know, but many parents of children who are later diagnosed with autism report excessive and persistent crying in the early years (this isn't universal, by any means: many others report an extremely calm baby), and while we didn't think anything of it then, retrospectively he fit the bill. At the time, though, we left it at "fussy baby."

I like to think that over the years I've developed a pretty good instinct for quickly assessing an infant for autism. Do they make eye contact? Smile? Coo? Show interest in people? Laugh? Make back-and-forth vocalizations? I've studied all the proper milestones and early signs, so I've asked myself a hundred times why it took me so long to notice that my own nephew was on the spectrum.

To be fair to myself, our family parties are chaotic, with tons of socializing and kids running around. Teddy didn't get wild or demand attention; he usually just played quietly with one of his favorite train sets. He didn't have any outward repetitive behaviors that were noticeable at a family party, so nothing immediately drew my attention, although his intense engagement with the trains would eventually lead to issues with sharing in preschool.

Then one day, another relative expressed concern that Teddy wasn't talking enough for a child who was about to turn two. She also was worried because he repeatedly turned her electric blanket on and off for hours and became upset when redirected. This repetitive behavior, coupled with his communication delay, caught my attention.

At our next family gathering, I made a point of joining Teddy on the floor, where he was playing with his train set, pushing the cars around the track. "Wow, awesome trains!" I said, but he didn't look up or acknowledge me. I pointed to the first one in his row and said, "Is that Thomas?" No response. I picked Percy up from the pile of cars Teddy wasn't using, and he immediately screamed, grabbed the car out of my hand, and put it back in its previous location. Teddy was nonverbal, didn't respond to a comment or point, and got upset when I attempted to join his play and change his routine. His behavior certainly fit the description of ASD.

I tried again to interact with him at the next family gathering, but every time I reached out, he reacted with the same deafening scream.

It was time to ask his parents to bring him in for an assessment.

The next week my suspicions were confirmed. No language. Check. No social interaction. Check. No interest in others. Check. Repetitive behaviors. Check. Lining up items. Check. No joint attention, no sharing of joy, no following a point, and on and on and on. Check, check, check, check.

Along with these symptoms of autism, Teddy had screaming meltdowns every time something didn't go his way.

As gently as I could, I suggested to his worried parents that we start a specialized program of support for autism.

THE ASSESSMENT

To confirm the diagnosis and secure services, two clinicians were assigned by the State of California's Regional Center System to meet with us at Teddy's home to observe him. (Note: Some states do not have, or no longer rely on, state agencies, as most states require insurance companies to provide coverage for autism services. Your pediatrician can guide you to, or assist with, a private evaluation. You can also contact your local school district for guidance and an evaluation to assess whether your child is eligible for services.) One of Teddy's evaluators was an experienced middle-aged preschool specialist; the other was an inexperienced early childhood special-ist, who walked in with a clipboard and immediately started shoot-ing off rote questions: "Did he meet his early milestones?" "When did he crawl? Sit up? Walk?"

They asked if we could try to get Teddy to talk. One of his favor-ite toys was a complicated set of ramps that balls could roll down, so I picked up one of the balls as it came through and modeled the word "ball" for him. Enormously upset that I had interrupted his activity, he screamed, picked up the maze of tunnels, and threw it on the floor. Parts scattered everywhere. The observers feverishly took notes on his "disruptive behaviors."

But while they were busily scribbling away, something incredible happened: Teddy quietly picked up the pieces and deftly reassem-bled the complicated toy—something I couldn't have done without an instruction manual.

In their final assessment, both observers mentioned Teddy's meltdowns, destructive behavior, absence of speech, and so on—but no one took note of this two-year-old's incredible ability to reassemble a toy with over a dozen separate pieces.

No kid his age could put together a complicated, multipiece toy that quickly without being super bright. In fact, most *adults* couldn't. He couldn't talk, but Teddy was *smart*.

And that's when I realized two important things.

First, if a child has disruptive behaviors, it can be hard to see past them. Years of research have shown that disruptive behaviors almost always have a communicative function, but it's difficult for people to recognize that in the moment.

Second, it's rare for professionals to take note of the strengths in children with ASD. The system simply isn't set up for that. As psychologists, speech pathologists, and special educators, we're trained to look for differences and deficits in the children we assess. That's what we provide services for and that's why children are referred to us. Further, the system has conditioned us to accentuate the negative: if the professional describes a child as "disruptive," "aggressive," and/or "tantrummy," the family is more likely to get services. Evaluations typically end up emphasizing the child's struggles and challenges and spend less time taking note of their strengths. And since these evaluations often take the lead in future discussions of the child's placements and goals, people often fail to take into account the huge potential and myriad capabilities of the child in question.

So, what changes when you realize how smart a child is?

A lot.

For one thing, you raise your expectations of the child's capabilities and potential. Having high expectations alone is a positive indicator for improvement in any child's quality of life, as more often than not, your child will rise to the occasion. As we'll discuss many times in this book, higher expectations have been shown repeatedly and scientifically to lead to better outcomes.

For another, once you start looking for signs of this brilliance, you'll notice how each strength gives you something to build on. Natural gifts and interests will give you new tools for engaging and teaching your child.

Recognizing a child's amazing talents—and making sure other people recognize them, too—can keep you focused on what matters: appreciating, loving, and supporting this unique and wonderful child you have right there in front of you. It will also prove to be an important tool in picking out the right programs for them.

Strengths and Interests

Throughout this book, we'll be encouraging you to "draw on your child's strengths and interests." There are a lot of reasons to do that, including:

- Motivation: Any person will be more interested and engaged in an activity if it includes an aspect that already speaks to them.

- Success: No one wants to spend their time feeling frustrated. If your child is building on an existing strength, they're far more likely to feel successful as they acquire new skills.

- Socialization: Your child is unlikely to be the only person their age who finds certain subjects fascinating. And we all know that common interests are the best foundation for support, friendships, and connection.

- Learning materials: If your child has already gathered a ton of information about a specific subject, you and their teachers will have helpful materials close at hand for teaching new skills: reading and math problems are way more fun if they include something that already speaks to you.

- Perseverance: Your child is likely to stay on task and attend longer if a subject or topic is of interest.

- Initiations: A common concern is that autistic individuals lack initiation (that is, reaching out to begin an interaction, as opposed to simply responding when someone else starts one), but if we draw upon their strengths and interests, they're likely to engage in way more initiations.

- Behavior: We rarely see behavior issues or interfering behaviors after we've taken a child's interests and strengths into consideration when planning a lesson or play session.

- Serendipitous learning: When tapping into a child's strengths, we see upticks in learning in unexpected areas, without any direct teaching. That is, when we set up the teaching so that the interactions are fun and enjoyable, they will be given the gift of "learning to learn," feeling comfortable enough to be open to absorbing new information.

- Affect: We all want happy kids. Studies show that if we take strengths and interests into account, children with ASD smile more often and show more interest in the learning activity, which creates a positive feedback loop.

- Parent satisfaction: Similarly, studies show that parents *also* smile more and show more positive engagement when their child's preferences are considered. They also report their role in teaching to be more enjoyable.

We're guessing you probably already have a good sense of your child's interests and the activities they enjoy, but in case you're feeling lost, here are some good places to start:

- TV shows, movies, or books that your child gravitates toward

- Toys they continually seek out

- Subjects they want to explore more deeply

- Skills they've surprised you by acquiring without being taught

- If they're verbal, conversations they have repeatedly

- Any activity that they willingly join or initiate, including everyday ones like cooking, putting puzzles together, drawing, etc.

- Physical activities, like riding a bike or trike, swinging, jumping on the trampoline

- Music, songs, or instruments that they enjoy

- Water play, sand, or other sensory activities that please them

- Academic subjects, such as numbers and letters, that they seek out on their own

And don't worry if their greatest interests differ from those of other children their age. The only thing that matters is that *your* child finds them appealing. Below are a few less-common activities that some of our children on the autism spectrum have enjoyed.

- Watching the car wash

- Opening and closing doors

- Smelling objects

- Watching and rewatching movie credits

- Sifting sand

- Sifting dried beans

- Learning to identify flags of different countries

- Collecting coins (from all over the world)

- Turning the lights on and off

As long as the interests and preferences aren't dangerous, don't let anyone tell you that they must be eliminated or ignored. When used to bolster the appeal of interactions, these interests don't increase, but they do become beneficial. For example, a preverbal child who enjoys ceiling fans can be taught words like "fan" and "on" and "go"—watching the fan becomes a learning experience, but one that the child is enjoying. Later on, much more complex language can be taught. Child choice matters. Make sure everyone makes use of it.

Teddy's Situation Is Far from Unique

A couple of years ago, my husband and I moved from Santa Barbara, where I had grown up, to work up north at Stanford University. Being in the heart of Silicon Valley has been fascinating—it's like a hub for brainy and inventive people. So, it's not surprising that their children are also brainy and inventive, including, of course, the ones on the spectrum.

I recently had a great conversation with an autistic preschooler, whose father owns a large tech company. It went something like this:

"Are we real?" he asked me.

I asked him to clarify.

"Are we in a dream?"

I asked for clarification again.

"Are we [characters] in a story that someone [else] is reading?"

This blew me away—a preschooler delving into philosophy and metaphysics! And these weren't uncommon questions for him.

Another preschooler I work with does struggle to socialize, but he is way, and I mean *way*, ahead of his peers in reading, spelling, and math. I wanted to teach him a few simple games that could be brought into the preschool to encourage peer interaction. I grabbed a pencil and paper and played a quick game of tic-tac-toe with him. Then I drew another grid to play again and put an O in the top left corner.

He got a little defiant smile on his face, covered the paper, and took his next turn without saying a word. When he handed it back to me, it said:

N O

TIC-TAC-TOE

He looked surprised when I burst out laughing, since he knew he had rejected my game and probably expected me to respond less positively, but when I congratulated him on his inventiveness, he smiled, pleased. I loved his unconventional—and undeniably clever—way of looking at things.

In these examples, while the children did struggle with social and communication skills, their brilliance was obvious. But as we saw in my own relative's case, often a child's intelligence is hidden and only discoverable with careful observation—which professionals may miss, since they tend to focus on assessing for areas with delays. In fact, most have been trained to look for weaknesses so they can implement programs to support those weaknesses, and in doing so, neglect to augment the child's strengths.

Nicolas, another student I worked with, was clearly super bright, consistently impressing me with his knowledge and insights. But in school he was unfocused and distracted, didn't complete his lessons, laughed or poked the other students, and screamed when peers didn't follow game rules.

When I asked why he didn't engage in classwork, Nicolas always replied with the same words: "Easy peasy." He was bored because the class was simply too easy for him. We will discuss solutions to this problem in detail later, but the important thing here is that the school didn't think of him as a gifted child who was being underserved; they considered him a "behavior problem." If they had recognized his brilliance right away, they could have given him extra work in a subject he enjoyed, which likely would have kept him busy and engaged.

Untapped Brilliance

By now you get the point: kids with ASD often reveal untapped brilliance if you know how to look for it. Unfortunately, too many bright kids are trapped in classes that do nothing to build on their strengths or to nurture their inherent intelligence. That's a big mistake.

And that's why we wrote this book: to remind parents, educators, and clinicians to look past a child's delays, challenges, and interruptive behaviors to the skills and wisdom lurking beneath them, to explain the mistakes made in assessments and program plans, and to share strategies for nurturing and unlocking a child's potential.

Stories

We'd like to share a few more stories about young people we've met through our work, all of whom needed a little extra support to reveal their hidden genius.

MIRANDA

Miranda was a nonverbal three-and-a-half-year-old. Although she had found other ways to communicate (such as leading people by the hand to what she wanted), her parents desperately and understandably wanted to hear her speak. The school and in-home specialists had suggested that she use a picture board for communication, as verbal communication seemed out of reach.

On one visit, her mother mentioned that when she sang a song to Miranda and paused, Miranda would sometimes fill in the next word. We had the mother show us, and, sure enough, when she sang "The Wheels on the Bus," Miranda could finish each line. The mother would sing the first part—"The babies on the bus go"—and stop, and Miranda would supply the "Waaaa waaaa waaaa." She could do that for every verse with clearly articulated words. This was huge—Miranda *could* talk when given the right context! She was laughing and smiling while her mother rocked her and sang, and we instantly knew music was the key to teaching her more words. She was capable of so much more than anyone had realized. This provided a good start for Miranda's first words. We added a few additional songs—"Old McDonald" was another favorite—and once she consistently was able to fill in the blanks, we began prompting words during everyday activities, using her favorite foods and games as the named objects. Words began emerging quickly.

Miranda is now able to communicate, using short sentences without prompts. The songs were a helpful, and perhaps necessary, bridge to her communication development. If it hadn't been for her mother's recognition of this strength, she might have remained non-verbal.

OLIVER

Oliver was diagnosed with "severe autism." We first met him when he accompanied his older brother, who had been diagnosed with Asperger syndrome, to the clinic. Oliver was eight years old, but his parents kept him strapped in a stroller: they claimed he got into too much trouble if they let him out. He didn't seem interested in interacting with us: when we asked him a question, he simply echoed the question back verbatim, rather than answering it.

One day I noticed that Oliver was staring avidly at the mini M&Ms we kept in our office. I decided to try something: I wrote down the name of a color on a small index card, showed him the color that corresponded to the word, then asked him if he could match it to the correct M&M. He matched it right away, so I gave him the mini-M&M. When I added the printed name of a second color, he was able to discriminate the two correct colors—he knew a lot more than he let on.

We kept going, adding in more colors and candies. Within about twenty minutes, he could match every written color to the correct candy. The next week we wrote a sentence—"Take a red candy"—and read it with him, pointing to each word. After a few times reading it through, he was able to read it by himself and follow the instruction. When we changed the color in the sentence, he was able to pick out the new color.

A few weeks later, we were adding numbers into the written instructions, such as, "Take two red candies and one blue candy," and he would read them out loud and then correctly follow through. It turned out Oliver—the boy who wouldn't answer questions—was a whiz at sight reading! He just needed the right motivation to demonstrate his talent. Within a few months, Oliver could read just about anything we put in front of him, and although his high interest in the tiny candies was useful and perhaps necessary for getting his reading started, his parents eventually faded out the candies—and the ability to read just kept growing.

STEVEN

Steven, a college student, received support from our team several times a week, which often focused on socialization. While sitting in the waiting room, he busied himself by going through our brochures and finding typographical or grammatical errors. It always surprised me that he could find a mistake on a brochure that had been repeatedly proofread. His parents were both attorneys and told us that he copyedited their legal briefs, court documents, and contracts for them.

Given how precisely he could read, it's not surprising that Steven did well in school, so when he got a failing grade in a class, we were all baffled. With his permission, we contacted the course instructor, who reported that Steven had done fine on the tests but had failed the group projects. We explained to the professor that making Steven repeat the course would just result in the same problem, and that it wasn't fair not to take into account his social differences, especially since he was so competent at the actual schoolwork. The professor relented and changed his grade to a pass.

As more and more people become aware of neurodiversity, individual differences, and the strengths and challenges that people on the autism spectrum face, reasonable accommodations can and should be made to help nurture their success. (Note: Colleges have no Individualized Educational Programs (IEPs), but they do have disability programs, and an increasing number have specialized programs for autistic students. Putting these services in place early on can be helpful for college students who may need extra support academically, socially, with time management, etc.)

JOEY

We recently visited a well-known center for autism. The longtime head of the program had run it using procedures developed in the 1960s, and the methods his staff used were frustratingly outdated. For instance, we saw a "therapist" pull out a picture flashcard of a glass of lemonade and ask, "Is lemonade sweet or sour?" The child they were working with said, "Sour," and the "therapist" shrugged her shoulders and said, "Yes, you could call it sour." Was there a right or wrong answer? It seemed to us that this child may have just learned to repeat the last word of the question. There was no learning going on here.

Next, we saw Joey, an adorable three-year-old boy with a small felt fedora roguishly tilted on his head, who was reportedly nonverbal. He was seated at a small table and the "therapist" working with him began a series of motor imitation exercises: "Do this," while she tapped her head; "Do this" while she tapped the table; "Do this" while she touched her nose, etc. Following each correct response, the "therapist" gave Joey a small candy. He was whining and fidgeting, and looked visibly upset throughout the activity, clearly not happily engaged or enjoying it.

After watching this for at least twenty minutes, we couldn't stand it anymore—this was going nowhere. We asked if we could work with Joey for a bit. Instead of rewarding him for the meaningless motor imitation, we grabbed one of the candies on the table that had been used for a reward for his imitation and modeled the word "candy." After we'd said it a few times, he repeated the word—at which point we immediately rewarded him with the candy. He also seemed interested in my long, colorful, beaded necklace, so I removed it and prompted the word "necklace," which he also repeated. I let him play with it a bit then pulled it toward me and asked, "What is it?" He instantly said, "Necklace." While not all children respond so quickly with first words, some do. After just ten minutes, he had said at least twenty words, astounding his entire group of providers, who had assumed he was incapable of talking and had been leaning on outdated teaching modes.

Program targets need to be meaningful. They need to be fun. And they need to be age appropriate. As we will discuss later, they should focus first and foremost on social communication—a delay in which is one of the two reasons a child is diagnosed as autistic. (And the other—interfering restricted and repetitive behavior—tends to fall out naturally once a child is socially communicating.) Imitating gestures and body movements won't translate to your child imitating words. Don't assume that because non-autistic children tend to develop one skill before another, in a generally predictable sequence, that your child with ASD must acquire skills in the same order. This can waste their valuable time and set them further behind.

COSMO

Cosmo was a six-year-old with ASD. His father reported that Cosmo once asked him, "Can you stop time?" Other intense and thoughtful Cosmo questions: "How can evolution form?" "What would the world be like if matter was made of photons and light was made of atoms?" "How does a gamma ray rip apart atoms?" Astonishingly, this brilliant little guy had a one-on-one aide at school because of issues with peers and inattention in class. Because so few children in his class had the range of knowledge that he did, we worked with the school to allow him to tutor his peers, and even take on an occasional "student teacher" role, when he could present some of his favorite topics (carefully chosen so they would interest the whole class). Once his friends experienced his helpfulness and intelligence, Cosmo became a respected and valued classmate, and peers started inviting him home to play.

In this case, his family and support staff knew just how bright Cosmo was, but his brilliance hadn't fully come out at school. By finding (fairly simple) avenues to allow that to happen, we were able to improve his overall social and academic experience.

SUMMARY

Let's work to change any negative messages to positives, leading with love. Write down or make a mental note of the answers to the questions below, and keep that list close to you (physically or mentally) at all times, because it's the key to moving your family forward and closer together:

- *What are my child's strengths?*

- *What does my child love to do/eat/watch?*

- *When is my child happiest?*

- *What does my child do best?*

- *What settings bring out the best in my child?*

- *What people bring out the best in my child?*

- *How does my child learn best?*

Share stories about your child's accomplishments, desires, and strengths. Let everyone know how amazing this kid is.

If an assessment, an Individualized Educational Program (IEP), a report, or a meeting about your child takes a downward turn, focusing on deficits or problems, speak up and change the narrative. If a tester tells you that your child's vocabulary was low on a standardized test or that your child's intelligence score was low, ask what words they *did* say or what skills they *did* show or what areas they *did* succeed at. Start with a strong focus on strengths and then discuss how to build upon these strengths to move forward. Talk about anything at home that negates reported deficits—maybe it's the time your child figured out how to unlock the door to go outside and play, or navigated your iPhone to play a favorite game, or asked to go for a ride in the car, or maybe it's that your child doesn't use interfering behaviors at home.

The main point is that too often professionals and community members look for differences—sadly, we're trained to do things that way—and these differences are usually problem areas, which means they don't focus on your child's strengths enough.

The most positive outcomes come from focusing on what your child is good at, enjoys, desires, and has accomplished. You know how amazing your child is: sharing that with the world and making it the main focus of any program leads to the greatest success—in every possible definition of that word.

CHAPTER 2

The Limits of Conventional Testing

More than a hundred years ago, scientists thought that measuring the size of someone's skull could determine how smart that person was—the larger the skull, the smarter the person. This sounds rightfully ridiculous to our modern ears, but the truth is that using IQ (intelligence quotient) tests for many children with ASD is about as useful as pulling out that tape measure, and yet these tests are still considered an integral part of our educational system.

The very first IQ test was developed in the early 1900s by Alfred Binet, a French psychologist. The purpose of this test was to identify those students who might benefit from some extra academic support. The goal was well intentioned, and the test has had its uses, but accumulating studies have revealed that testing often results in an inaccurate (usually skewing too low) estimation of abilities—especially for students on the autism spectrum.

Standardized tests are plentiful and can test IQ, language, academics, and many other areas. The reasons for testing are varied, but tests are frequently used to diagnose a child with a learning difference, by comparing their scores with those of their peers, an often necessary precursor to accessing services.

It's important to note that there are many things that standardized tests *can't* evaluate, such as problem solving, creativity, and artistic ability. Also, at this date, standardized tests won't assess accumulated knowledge in specialized areas of interest, so if your child is extraordinarily knowledgeable in a specific area, you need to let the school know that. (If your child is in high school and excelling in a specific academic area, AP (advanced placement) exams in high school might pick this up, but only if the strength is in a subject offered by a college.)

Many professionals use testing when they have a sense that a student is either noticeably gifted or noticeably struggling. You tend to find what you're looking for and, for those who have been struggling, if enough tests are given, they likely *will* eventually show an area of challenge. We all have strengths and weaknesses, and weaknesses will show up, if someone is determined to find them.

We've seen many parents get overwhelmed by unexpected or negative test results. And if a parent is already experiencing concern, a bad test result can be the final straw that sends them into a tailspin. Learning about a poor test score can also affect a child's self-esteem and self-confidence, especially if they sense a parent's or teacher's concern.

One young child we know was told that he scored 100 on an IQ test. Believing that the score indicated 100 percent correct, rather than the median level of performance, he ran around boasting that he had a perfect score, only to be crushed when he was told that actually, it was an average one.

We need to stop emphasizing negatives and start focusing on the positives. *Every* child has strengths. These should be emphasized, described, discussed, and expanded. It is extremely important for teachers, administrators, parents, and others working with the child to see the whole child, not just test results, since testing is unlikely to draw out an autistic child's strengths. All strengths, no matter how small, should be listed in an evaluation, so everyone can get a well-rounded picture of who your child is, and not just see them as a single negative test result. We'll discuss this later at greater length; for now, let's start with a discussion of some of the various reasons for unreliably low scores, including communication challenges, interfering behaviors, and low motivation. Next, we'll discuss the problems that arise from poor test results, and how they often lead to low goals and low expectations. And, finally, we'll discuss the ways to get around these problems and help people see just how bright and capable your child is, no matter what a standardized test says.

First, it's important to understand that test administrators are required to follow specific protocols so they don't end up unintentionally skewing the results.

Test protocols (or instructions on how to give the test) do not allow testers to "feel their way through" a situation by giving a struggling child cues or help: they have to follow the protocols, to keep things fair and even. Being a tester is a bit like being a poker player: you don't want to give anything away. You aren't supposed to react in any way if a child gets an answer right or wrong, and you have to hide your own knowledge of the correct answer—children can pick up on any and all cues, like a little smile after a correct answer, a furtive glance at a picture, or a frown when an answer is way off.

A tester *is* allowed to encourage participation and attention: you may compliment the child or give a sticker or other reward for nice sitting or good trying, but the rewards have to be distributed evenly across both right and wrong answers.

Unfortunately, this strict methodology may make testing more challenging for children with differences.

For example, say we give a test that assesses memory, and we list a string of numbers, but then realize that the student wasn't paying attention. Testing protocol dictates that we cannot repeat the string of numbers, because hearing the numbers twice might give the child an unfair advantage over those who only heard the numbers once. But if the child clearly wasn't attending or has some type of learning challenge that might make repetition helpful, their inability to remember the numbers might have nothing to do with their intelligence. Repeating the string of numbers for them might have proven that, under the correct conditions, they're capable of memorizing them. In short, sometimes tests just aren't an accurate representation of a child's abilities.

Interpreting Tests

Most standardized test manuals include an evaluation table that helps you locate a student's score in the bell curve of test scores drawn from a large random sample. The student's results are therefore not based on their percentage of correct answers, but rather where that percentage falls in relation to the "normative" sample. For example, if a child scores at the 50th percentile, this means they are smack dab in the middle of where the normative sample fell, or else right on the median for their age or grade level. Above the 50th percentile means their score was higher than the average, and below the 50th percentile means their score was lower than the average score of the sample. At some point, as the score moves further away from the middle, a child is considered either to be advanced in the tested area or to have a "disability."

So, theoretically, a test score allows you to see how significantly challenged a child might be—or conversely, how gifted they might be. What makes it even more reductive is that, for many tests, technology advances allow a tester to simply input the child's answers into a computer program and then receive an automatic score with a detailed description of the student's strengths and weaknesses. A lot of conclusions can be drawn from something that might not be that accurate or specific.

We aren't saying that tests are never helpful, because they often can be. But we *are* saying that they may not be an accurate estimate of your child's ability, especially if your child is on the autism spectrum.

These are many reasons why any child—and especially an autistic child—might perform below their abilities on a test. We explore them below.

ATTENTION ISSUES

I once visited an elementary school classroom when the teacher was in the middle of administering a class-wide IQ test to see which students qualified for the school's gifted program. (Schools differ in how they assess for the gifted program, and generally a number of factors are considered; however, this school happened to assess all students in the second grade using a standardized IQ test.) While I was there, I saw a lot of the students staring out the window, playing with their pencils, chewing on the erasers, peeking in their desks, and so on.

None of the children appeared to be completely off task, but a lot of them weren't entirely *on* task either, and many were engaging in behaviors that were likely to be distracting and take their attention away from the test.

So, here's the important question:

What was really being tested here—*intelligence* or *focus*?

If you're staring out the window or playing with your pencil when you're supposed to be reading test questions and filling out answer bubbles, you probably won't make it into the gifted program, no matter what level you read at or how thoughtful you can be when you're interested in a subject. Schools that recognize this will often also test or consider children individually for gifted programs based on a teacher's recommendation, but many don't take this extra step. If a child isn't answering the test questions, there's no way of knowing what they know.

Children with ASD are highly likely to have attention issues, especially when something isn't related to their interests—and standardized tests are seldom based on any one child's interests. But it would be a mistake to conflate their lack of attention with a lack of intelligence. I've worked with many children who appear to be spacing out during an entire class period, and who can't answer a single question about that specific topic, but then when I've asked them what they were thinking about, their thoughts were complex and sophisticated.

Once I was administering a test to a young student with autism and asked him to point to pictures of different vocabulary words. He pointed to a few, and then simply stopped responding to me. Rather than assuming that he had reached his potential, I asked him why, and he gestured at the pictures and said, "This is stupid. Everyone knows what those are."

Another child's dad told us that his autistic son was rolling on the floor during his entire IQ test and the test administrator was running after him the whole time. How could that test have accurately measured his son's intelligence?

Additionally, many standardized tests are timed. If a child daydreams during that limited time, takes a while to transition, or simply has more important things to think about, they may not score as well as a child who's responding with immediate and focused attention.

INTERFERING BEHAVIORS

Restricted and repetitive behaviors, which are often associated with ASD, such as flapping, clapping, body rocking, and repetitive noises, can interfere with test taking.

Additionally, if a child tends to show behavior issues when confronted with an unpleasurable task (issues which can range from aggression to simple noncompliance), this can interfere with accurate testing. (It's important to mention here that this doesn't have to happen. Please read chapter 4, "Tackling Behaviors That Can Dim Your Child's Bright Light," for more about this.)

When children demonstrate these behaviors, they can be challenging to test, and their scores are more likely to reflect their level of interfering behavior than their level of intelligence—the higher the level of interfering behaviors, the more likely it is they won't respond to test questions. So testing any child with interfering behaviors is unlikely to reveal their true cognitive, academic, or language levels—and since children on the autism spectrum often have these sorts of behaviors, once again that means that they're at a high risk for inaccurate test results.

LACK OF INTEREST

A young child who takes a test is unlikely to be thinking about how a good test score might help their GPA or get them academically fast-tracked. There's no inherent motivation for a child to want to take a test, but a lot of kids *do* enjoy the social interaction and praise that a good tester will make sure are part of the experience, and will, as a result, want to respond and please them.

But children on the autism spectrum don't tend to be as socially motivated. They may not find the same level of reward in praise, smiles, and social approval that most non-autistic children do. You can see how that plays out in language acquisition: most non-autistic kids' first words are "mama" or "dada," "dis?" or "dat?" (a shortened form of the question "What's this? or "What's that?") because those are social words that bring them attention. But autistic children usually have first words that are practical, related to things they want ("juice," "train," etc.). They're communicating more to get their needs met than to initiate a social interaction.

Similarly, for many children, a parent's praise is meaningful, but for a child on the autism spectrum, a hug and an "I'm proud of you!" may not mean as much as, say, free time to go on the computer or talking about a preferred interest. So why bother with tests just because the teacher and your parent care about them? That's simply not a huge motivation for many of these kids, especially since there's often very little else in a standardized test to hold their interest. The research shows that all kids learn faster if teaching is based around their interests, and those interests tend to be limited or specialized for children on the autistic spectrum—and unlikely to be found scattered throughout standardized test questions. Test questions are not, of course, geared toward any specific interests, but the test writers do try to reference things they assume children of the testing age will enjoy thinking about, and autistic kids may not be as likely to find those things fascinating. Also, children who are more socially inclined may be driven to perform well for praise and attention or may simply take an interest in looking at pictures or other test items and interacting with an adult, but this may not be the case for an autistic child.

Research has also shown that students perform best when they experience a connection between a behavior and its outcome: a connected natural outcome makes the behavior "meaningful" to the child. Actually, this is true for all of us, at any age. For example, if we write a shopping list and it helps us remember the items we need to purchase, our exercise of writing was meaningful. On the other hand, if we write a shopping list and don't go to the store, writing the list was a waste of time and we might lose interest in writing any more shopping lists. Furthermore, if we have to write a shopping list every day but *never* use it, odds are good we'll start to want to actively avoid wasting any time writing a list. Worse yet, if we're writing a shopping list that we *know* is never going to be used, and someone is standing over us correcting our spelling or telling us that our handwriting isn't legible—i.e., criticizing the way we're writing this useless list and making the effort to write it stressful and unpleasant—we're *really* going to dislike that activity and will do whatever we can not to engage in it.

Now let's apply this to an activity a student might be asked to participate in—say, taking a standardized test. From the very first engagement with the tester, a student on the autism spectrum may be set up for failure rather than success.

Many tests begin with a few training examples, which don't count toward the score but allow the tester to make it clear what will be asked of the child. The tester might say something like "Point to the picture of sleeping," and if the child doesn't respond correctly, the tester is still allowed to provide some instruction, or prompts.

Unfortunately, it's quite likely that a tester's response to any incorrect or nonexistent answer will feel negative, even reproving. The tester may not even be aware that by redirecting or correcting the child, they're creating an uncomfortable or unpleasant environment, but no one enjoys being told they've failed at a task, and in this particular situation, that unfortunately tends to be the conveyed message.

On the other hand, if the child *does* get the hang of the task from the practice examples, what's their reward? The tester moves right along to the actual test, and dives into asking many more questions! That's not a great reward for someone who doesn't see the meaning in this exercise in the first place. At this point the student might understandably wonder, *What's the point of continuing to respond? I'll just be asked to answer another question and another, and none of them mean anything to me.*

To sum up, the fact that social differences and social withdrawal form one of autism's main diagnostic areas means that kids on the autism spectrum don't tend to be inherently interested in pleasing an adult for social rewards, the way a more engaged, non-autistic child might be. (However, please note that there are complexities to this statement, which we will discuss later.) Without the built-in social desire for engagement and praise, kids on the autism spectrum need any task to be meaningful in and of itself—who can blame them if they find testing questions irrelevant to their lives? And even if one test question happens to grab their attention, the tester will move quickly to the next question, which again may be uninteresting. Restricted interests, often in unusual, even unconventional areas, are likely to mean that an autistic test taker isn't finding much to engage them in a test designed for more conventional tastes and interests. Add to this higher levels of interfering behaviors when something is uninteresting to them, and less of a desire for adult approval, and there are quite a few reasons why students on the spectrum are less likely to excel at a standardized test than their non-autistic peers.

"CEILINGS"

For most tests, there's a start point, usually based on the child's age, and then the testing will continue until the child isn't able to answer questions correctly, at which point the test is now considered to be above the child's ability level. That point is referred to as the *ceiling*. A ceiling can be based on a specific number of wrong answers in a row or so many out of so many, depending on the testing instructions.

Students on the autism spectrum tend to have widely varying levels of skills—they may test above what would be expected for their chronological age in some areas and far below in others. This can result in longer testing sessions to reach a ceiling since the child may perform unevenly—in other words, while a lot of kids might reach a level where they consistently get answers wrong, the student on the autism spectrum may occasionally get a question in an area they excel in, answer that one correctly, and have to keep going because the "ceiling" hasn't been met. So, the test is dragging on, but they're also getting a lot wrong, which can be draining and is highly likely to be unenjoyable.

Another problem is that, when some children hit a level where a lot of the questions are difficult, they get so frustrated they don't want to continue, even if they're capable of getting many more correct answers. We tested one elementary school child who was breezing through a test until he was stumped several times in a row, at which point he felt so frustrated that he refused to continue taking the test. So, his final score reflected more about his frustration levels than about his intelligence or ability.

HAVING AN OFF DAY

It's generally recommended that all children be tested across at least two days. That way, if they didn't have a good night's sleep, skipped breakfast, or were just "off" one day in a way that might affect their test results, any inconsistent results between that day and the other day might lead the tester to surmise that the lower scores underestimated the child's ability. But realistically, many testers—especially in cash-strapped schools or in clinics with long wait lists and designated appointment times—can't be that flexible. If a child has a set time for an evaluation, it's likely to take place as scheduled, even if it feels like it's not an ideal time for that child to take that test. Everyone has an off day once in a while, especially students on the autism spectrum—who tend to have sleep difficulties—and if that day is when an evaluative test is being given, that student might test below their actual abilities.

HIGH LANGUAGE DEMANDS

Many standardized tests assess receptive vocabulary (words a child can understand), expressive vocabulary (words a child can say), receptive language (understanding the meaning of what's said to them), and expressive language (using words to communicate meaning, including wants, needs, thoughts, and ideas). In addition to those specific language tests, more general IQ tests often test a combination of verbal and nonverbal abilities.

Now remember, social communication is one of the core diagnostic criteria of ASD—in fact, research has long shown that a common reason for parents first seeking an assessment is a delay in spoken words.

So, we know that many children diagnosed with autism have speech and language delays and/or challenges, but then we administer tests to them that require verbal abilities to perform well. Is it surprising that their test results often don't seem to line up with the intelligence their families have seen in action?

We do have a variety of tests of *nonverbal* intelligence, and often autistic children perform extremely well on these. Unfortunately, they aren't commonly administered. Most psychologists only give one IQ test, and they tend to favor ones that have both verbal and nonverbal sections, since they cover a broad range. And, of course, the IQ score reflects the total test, not just the nonverbal sections, so a child who scores much higher in those sections will see those scores flattened out by the other sections.

With nonverbal intelligence tests, even the *directions* are nonverbal (shown in pictures and nonverbal demonstration), so verbal abilities won't come into play when assessing cognitive levels. Once we eliminate the verbal component of testing, many of the kids in the ASD community do astonishingly well, demonstrating strong skills in things like completing patterns and classifying similar objects, supporting the fact that language difficulties can result in inaccurately low scores for our kids.

UNEQUAL PREPPING

A school psychologist friend once tested a child whose father also happened to be a psychologist. The child had been referred by her teacher to test for the school's gifted and talented program, undoubtedly after encouragement from the father. During the test, the child innocently admitted that her father had gone over the test items with her the night before—an action which, not surprisingly, can have a huge impact on outcome.

The truth is that many parents prep their children for standardized testing in a myriad of ways that can range from enrolling them in online test prep programs to simply stressing the importance of doing well. Any of these can be a variable in higher test scores, and if prepping isn't applied consistently across the board to all the children taking the same test, it can give an unfair advantage to those who get it.

We're not saying prepping is a bad thing—in fact, we highly recommend it for children with learning differences and other challenges (read ahead in this book for plenty of information about the value of "priming"). We're just saying that it's important to be aware that prepping can skew or distort test results.

LACK OF PRIOR EXPOSURE TO THE CONTENT

One of the issues with all tests—but especially language-based ones—is that they rely heavily on experience or exposure. For instance, if a test includes the word "stirrup," it's quite possible that only someone who's spent time around horses will recognize it. Similarly, if you don't go to museums, you might not have encountered the words "exhibit" or "statues." And so on. Also, tests aren't updated all that often, so pictures of common items like phones, toothbrushes, and frozen meals may not look like the ones the child sees every day. One common vocabulary test was using a picture of a typewriter long after the world had switched to computers.

It should be clear that the importance of exposure to a wide range of knowledge is likely to affect kids with ASD negatively, since they tend to have restricted interests and go on fewer outings than other children.

We once worked with a little guy who was super interested in toilets. Yes, toilets. He actually taught everyone a lot about them, and knew some vocabulary words we hadn't previously encountered, like cistern, float ball, S-bend, and up flush. He had an amazing grasp of a very specific vocabulary—but one that (regrettably for him) wasn't likely to appear on standardized tests.

Another child we worked with was interested in Botts' dots—the little raised reflectors on freeways and roads that provide auditory feedback if you stray over the line—something no one in our clinic had previously given much thought to (despite many of us having driven over them a shameful number of times). This boy knew about every kind and color but was most interested in their chemical composition—which he felt could be improved.

Similarly, a four-year-old child we work with loves drains. His awesome dad has helped him study drainage systems, and he has a strikingly large drainage vocabulary and understanding, one that could put most plumbers to shame.

Despite mastery of these specific vocabularies, none of these children tested well on standardized vocabulary tests, and it's no surprise—these tests aren't likely to pull vocabulary from these specialized areas. If a child has an enormous vocabulary about toilets, Botts' dots, or drains, but then scores in the bottom 5th, 10th, or 15th percentile on a standardized vocabulary test, that test tells us nothing about that child.

CAN INTELLIGENCE BE MEASURED?

IQ tests are wildly popular: you probably won't find a school in the country or a psychology clinic in the world that doesn't use them and draw conclusions from their results. And yet study after study have reported that IQ scores are not an accurate measure of intelligence, and that no single measure can define or quantify a person's intelligence.

It's been shown and studied: IQ tests measure *circumstance* rather than innate intelligence. They are biased against children from lower socioeconomic backgrounds; wealthy children score higher than those from low-income backgrounds.

There is no gene for abstract reasoning, reading, or math—a child's skill level in these areas is more likely to reflect their environment and exposure than any inherent abilities.

What's particularly worrisome is that many people who use IQ testing also believe that IQs are static—that, so long as you use an age-appropriate test, the results will be accurate for the lifetime of the individual. This can mean that a child who tests badly at an early age, for whatever reason, may be regarded as having a "low IQ" for the rest of their academic life. But we know that test-taking abilities and behaviors can change wildly over time, and, as we've shown, could have a huge effect on the results of the test. The idea of a "static IQ" is simply a myth.

Binet himself did not believe that his own psychometric instruments designed for testing IQ could or should be used to measure a single, permanent, inborn level of intelligence. He was well aware of the limitations of his test and suggested that intelligence is far too broad a concept to quantify with a single number derived from a single test. That was never his intention. Despite this, the concept of being able to measure intelligence has been accepted for hundreds of years, and, unfortunately for those who don't test well, standardized tests are used for educational placement decisions, curricular goals, and social goals.

Low test scores can lead to children being excluded from participating in certain settings and activities: they can provide a case for exclusion from mainstream general education settings and result in IEP goals that minimize academic and social engagement opportunities. A child who scores low on an early IQ test may be placed in a more restrictive special education class and/or given low academic goals. But if the test is measuring something other than actual knowledge—as it was in all those examples we described above— the students' goals might be partially, or even fully developed around test scores that didn't measure their intelligence at all. As a result, these potentially bright kids might spend years not being appropriately challenged—even, tragically, not really learning anything at all.

We know someone, a successful adult now, who as a preschooler was a bit of a "wild child," roaming unsupervised around his neighborhood. When he started kindergarten, all the incoming students were given IQ tests. The only thing he remembers about taking the test was that the first question was so silly and easy that he punched the examiner in the stomach and ran away. Shortly thereafter, his parents received a letter informing them that their son would be placed in a special education class for children with severe "disabilities," because he had scored zero on the IQ test.

His parents wisely insisted on having him retested and made sure he answered enough questions to achieve the score required for a general education class. But if his parents had been more passive, he might well have stayed in special education, and his entire education would have gone down a different path.

Would his special ed teachers eventually have noticed that he didn't belong there? There's no way to know. His boredom with a far too easy curriculum might have led to more problem behaviors, or the teachers might have been too busy with challenging pupils to think much about the ones who didn't need extra support. He might well have slipped through the cracks and never found a path back to a regular classroom.

This is someone who went on to become a university professor— but who scored a zero on an IQ test that could have erroneously determined his first school placement. And this kind of thing is still happening.

THE ROSENTHAL EFFECT

A well-known research study by Robert Rosenthal and Lenore Jacobson in 1966 identified some students as gifted, supposedly based on IQ tests, information which the researchers then relayed to the students' teachers—who didn't know that their "gifted" students had actually been chosen at random, independent of any test scores. At the end of the study, the students labeled "academic bloomers" had performed much better academically than their fellow students during the school year.

Why might this happen? Well, studies show us that teachers may call more frequently on the students they think well of, give them more instruction and more feedback, provide them with additional academic materials, smile or nod more often when they speak, and so on. All of these interactions encourage the students and make them feel seen and comfortable in the classroom, which can lead to higher achievement. This effect seems to be especially strong in the early years of school.

In short, teacher behavior can change based on expectations; if they identify certain students as exceptional (based on testing or evaluations) they're more likely to attend to those students—and all of these extra interactions help students improve. This is the "Rosenthal" or "Pygmalion" effect. (We'll discuss all of this in more depth in chapter 5, "Working with Schools to Nurture Your Child's Brilliance.") The important thing here is to understand how an inaccurately low test score might drag down your child's potential if a teacher places too much emphasis on it.

The results of this study suggest that if a teacher believes a student is likely (or unlikely) to succeed, independent of test scores, the student will perform better (or worse) over the course of that school year. That is, if a teacher thinks a student is intelligent, the teacher will challenge and engage the student, but if the teacher thinks the student lacks potential, the teacher might not bother to try, and the student's performance will reflect this expectation. Some later studies question to what extent this is consistently true, but there's plenty of evidence to suggest that teachers have trouble rising above their own expectations and biases when it comes to interacting with their students.

We worked with a young autistic student who had difficulties with social interactions (but was on an improving trend) and who was very bright. The family moved, and instead of describing the child as having a "disability," they told the new administration that he was very gifted. Once his teachers categorized him as gifted, instead of as having a "disability," they gave him additional assignments, more attention, and increased academic feedback. They also recruited him to help some of his classmates, which provided him with a friend group of peers. Tapping into strengths can make a world of difference for a child.

What This Means for Your Child

We think you can see why the reliance on testing is worrisome for parents of kids with ASD—if a test ends up assessing behavior or verbal skills instead of their child's true abilities (and most do), it's possible no one at school will ever realize how bright their child really is.

In 1997, we published a study that our research team titled "Variables Related to Differences in Standardized Test Outcomes for Children with Autism" in the *Journal of Autism and Developmental Disorders*. We selected six children who, according to the schools, had a lot of interfering behaviors *and* had received extremely low IQ and language scores. We had a suspicion that the scores might not be completely accurate, simply because the children were challenging to test. All of the students had been placed in special education as a result of their poor test scores.

We observed each child, interviewed the parents, and noted behaviors that might have interfered with responding on the test. For example, Johnny spent most of his day talking like a cartoon character—and continued doing this while a tester was trying to give instructions. Kyle got so excited when he saw a picture of something he liked during a test that he would name or point to the item, even if it wasn't the correct answer to the question. Jack engaged in repetitive behaviors, which interfered with his ability to respond to the test questions. Cara screamed and ran away when we asked her to sit at the table. Mason had a few favorite books that he carried everywhere and would leaf through them when he was supposed to be paying attention; if his books were taken away, he had a meltdown that could last for an hour or more. And when Harry received a test instruction, he would cry, punch, kick, and scream—anything to get out of cooperating, unless his mother or babysitter was around; then, he was calm.

Our team decided to try other ways to test these students, taking into account their behavioral patterns. The results were decidedly different from the previous tests results. We learned a lot from this about how to help kids with ASD nurture their abilities and intelligence, all of which we will share in future chapters. For now, let's talk specifics about how to take on the challenge of testing our intelligent and talented students as fairly and accurately as possible.

Getting Fair and Accurate Assessments

Below, we're going to talk about how you can help your child have a more accurate assessment. We realize that we talk quite a bit about requiring your school to make concessions and accommodations, and we know it can feel like a daunting task to approach school professionals to ask for these things, which is why, in chapter 5, "Working with Schools to Nurture Your Child's Brilliance," we will discuss how to advocate successfully for your child. Always remember that no one knows your child better than you do, which makes you the true expert in any situation involving them, and that you have a right to make requests based on that fact alone.

ASK FOR A SPECIFIC TEST (OR KIND OF TEST)

If your district requires standardized testing for securing special education services, choose the ones that are most likely to bring out the best in your child with ASD. As we mentioned earlier, IQ tests are still widely used, despite all the evidence that they measure a child's circumstance and background more than they do a child's potential or intelligence. In addition, the most commonly given IQ tests have both verbal and nonverbal components. An autistic child is likely to have the most difficulty with verbal portions of the test, since communication delays are one of the criteria for diagnosing autism, and strengths tend to concentrate in nonverbal areas. Testing the very areas that are challenging for a child, such as comprehension and reasoning concepts, using spoken language that they struggle to understand, is likely to set that child up for a low score. But that same child might score in the average range, or even excel, in nonverbal areas that don't require spoken language for evaluation. Often people assume that children with a lower overall IQ score will perform poorly across the board. It makes a difference if someone is underestimating a perfectly capable child who simply has difficulty with verbal communication—educational placement and goals may differ if a child is considered to have an "intellectual disability." In contrast, higher scores on a nonverbal IQ test that measures a child's aptitude using visual and hands-on reasoning may demonstrate a child's strengths, leading to higher expectations, helpful information for future teachers, and access to the same educational programs as children who test in the average or above average range on a verbal IQ test. If you're concerned that your child may not have the language to do well on common IQ tests, there *are* alternatives, such as picture-based or nonverbal tests. You can, and should, ask for a completely nonverbal IQ test if your child is better at visual tasks.

Another option, if you don't want your child to be stuck with a score that underestimates their abilities, is to see if your school district will allow the school psychologist to ballpark your child's IQ. Adaptive functioning, or how well an individual performs in daily life, is not necessarily measured accurately by an IQ score, but can be assessed through structured interviews with parents, teachers, or care providers, which are likely to provide more accurate details of your child's capabilities. The school psychologist can look at the whole picture of who your child is, not just at a single test score.

PROVIDE INFORMATION AND INSIGHT

If your child is getting evaluated by a school or program, the process will probably include a variety of standardized tests and observations. These may be used to help determine whether your child has a learning difference, if your child qualifies for special education services or placement, where your child's knowledge is compared with that of other children, what the type of difference might be, and how to adjust the curriculum, if necessary. These are designed to better help your child succeed, and many tests can be repeated to assess progress and development. Tell the tester what motivates your child, so their interests can be used as an incentive during testing. If your child sits well for short periods of time, but not long ones, let the tester know that they should conduct the tests in short bursts over many days.

The number of observations included in the evaluation will vary depending on the evaluator—some choose to include a lot of supplemental information, and others rely heavily (and sometimes even solely) on standardized test scores. To ensure that your child's strengths are taken into account, you can provide advance information to the examiners about any positive behaviors that may not be seen during the testing. If your child has a special interest, be sure the evaluator includes detailed information about their knowledge in this area, which is likely to exceed other children's.

Some autistic children excel in areas that are unexpected for their age group and therefore not likely to be part of any test. For example, if your preschooler can sing whole songs, knows their numbers and letters, and reads some words, inform the tester. Alert the tester to *anything* that your child can do that the school may be unaware of.

If you communicate your child's strengths through written notes, video clips, or in person, you'll help any assessor understand your child and know what to look for. Make sure the tester knows your child's strengths, areas of excellence, motivators, and skills, and that they're all included in the final report.

MAKE THE TEST MORE COMFORTABLE FOR YOUR CHILD

As we mentioned earlier, kids with ASD often aren't intrinsically motivated to work hard and do well on standardized assessments.

But there *are* ways to make the overall experience more relaxing and appealing to them. We've listed a few below.

1. **REQUEST AN EXPERIENCED EXAMINER.** We published a study in the *Journal of Autism and Developmental Disorders* showing the vast differences in IQ and language scores that can result, depending on whether or not an examiner individualizes a test, particularly when the child has interfering behaviors. It's critical that the examiner have experience with students with ASD and understand that they may not put forth a full effort if they're not motivated—and that they're not likely to be motivated by the same things that a non-autistic student might be.

2. **MAKE SURE THE EXAMINER HAS A GOOD RAPPORT WITH YOUR CHILD.** That can make a huge difference in whether your child performs at the height of their abilities or just disengages. Take a look at your child's affect with the examiner: you want to see enjoyment, engagement, and an absence of stress. Is the examiner engaging with them, offering their favorite toys and activities to warm up, and trying to figure out what will motivate them? If the examiner simply moves straight to testing without developing some rapport, the child may not perform as well. If you feel like the examiner isn't connecting with your kid, you should request a different examiner.

3. **KEEP THE TESTING SHORT.** Tests for language, cognitive functioning, and academic skills often take many hours to administer, and autistic students may not be able to focus for that long on something with no built-in motivation for them (as we discussed earlier). Once the student loses patience with and interest in the process, they're unlikely to concentrate hard enough to work out the correct answers or even respond at all. Shorter test periods can make the process less stressful and are

likely to lead to more successful results, so ask for testing to be
broken up. While tests have guidelines as to how they should
be administered, almost all can be given in multiple sittings.
Remember, most tests keep on going until your child misses a
certain number in a row or fails a certain percentage of times.
This ensures that the child's ability to answer the test items has
been exceeded, but it can mean that the testing goes on longer
than your child can comfortably manage. Give your child the
best chance by asking that only one test be administered a day (or
even just part of a test) and/or requesting that the examiner have
a time limit in place, based on your knowledge of how long your
child can comfortably sit and attend.

4. **MAKE SURE YOUR CHILD IS AT THEIR BEST.** If there is some reason
   your child may be having an off day (some kids struggle to adjust
   to being back to school on Mondays, for example, or maybe
   your child is recovering from a cold, didn't sleep well the night
   before, etc.), ask to reschedule the test, to give your child the
   best possible chance to have their skills truly and accurately
   measured.

5. **MAKE USE OF RESTRICTED INTERESTS.** Restricted interests are
   an inherent part of the diagnosis of autism, and you can turn
   that into a huge positive when your child is being tested. Many
   individuals have accumulated a vast amount of information about
   topics that aren't likely to be asked about during standardized
   testing. There's no question that a well-rounded vocabulary,
   an ability to make small talk, and an interest in others are all
   important skills, but so is an ability to dive deeply into a specific
   subject. In fact, later in life, restricted interests can guide college
   majors, employment, leisure activities, and social opportunities.
   They can also be used during teaching, as we'll discuss in later
   chapters. The antiquated idea that restricted interests should be

ignored or decreased has been wiped away by repeated studies showing that using these strengths can be valuable for academic gain and socialization. We worked with a child who was reported to have "very low verbal skills with only a few short sentences." We asked for a reassessment and sent in his favorite book on dinosaurs. Not only did he produce long and complex sentences, but he revealed an enormous vocabulary related to dinosaurs. So, the fact was that he had very well-developed and complex language—just not with the materials that were available in the examiner's room.

Not only should these interests be mentioned and assessed, but access to interest-related activities can also be used as an enjoyable reward during a break, or after a designated time period, or following a specific number of questions answered. Make sure the final report showcases these strengths in detail. They matter.

6. **FAMILIARIZE YOUR CHILD WITH THE TEST.** We worked with a student who had memorized a ton of facts but had a difficult time understanding what was required of him on tests. Simply previewing the *directions* on each test—not the answers, of course, just the directions—made the difference for him between failing and passing with flying colors. Ask specifically which tests will be given and Google them. While unlicensed people can't purchase many tests and give an unfair advantage to their child, most websites will have some general information, like how long it takes to give the test, the general format of the test, whether there's writing involved, and the instructions they're likely to use. Knowing a bit about the test can help you identify any potential pitfalls and make a plan to avoid them. One child we worked with was asked to match pictures. The examiner said, "Which goes with which?" while showing him a few of the cards. He responded with, "There are no witches there." Had he understood the meaning of *which* in the context

of the activity, he would have been able to respond to the test demands accordingly.

7. **MAKE THE PROCESS AS STRESS-FREE AS POSSIBLE.** Some students perform better if a parent or some other familiar person is in the room, so that might be worth arranging. Others have a special little comforting object that helps them relax—just be sure that any special object doesn't interfere with responding. We recently tested a child who repetitively banged a stuffed toy on the furniture. He refused to give it up when we began to evaluate him, but fortunately the babysitter was there and told us that he knew to hand it to her when she counted down from five—and that worked for us, too. (This also illustrates beautifully how important it is to listen and take advice from those who know a child well.)

PUT ANY TEST RESULTS IN CONTEXT

If you think the test results don't accurately portray your child's abilities, make sure the final draft of the report clearly acknowledges that many children with ASD have difficulty taking tests and that any tests administered may underestimate the child's true knowledge and abilities. It's vitally important that anyone making classroom assignments understand that these tests can be inaccurate in evaluating an autistic student's intelligence, language, and academic potential—you don't want your bright child placed in a classroom that won't challenge or engage them.

Research has demonstrated that many students, especially those with interfering behaviors, can have extremely variable test results, depending on their frame of mind and engagement while taking the test. We worked with one child who the school determined had a "moderate" cognitive delay, scoring around 50 (considered in the "intellectual disability" range) on the IQ test. We retested him, giving him frequent breaks, and asking him to repeat the instructions back to us to make sure he was attending, and guess what? He scored in the average range. Once again, that first time, they weren't testing his intelligence, just his behavior.

No administrator or teacher should put too much faith in standardized test results when it comes to students with ASD or rely solely on them for class placements or goals.

ASK FOR INPUT FROM OBSERVATIONS

For most autistic children, behavioral observations should constitute the bulk of any evaluation—it's a far more natural and ultimately accurate way to gauge a child's abilities than sitting them down and testing them. And by all means make sure that any observations include time spent noting your child's strengths, not just any perceived weaknesses.

For academic areas, make sure your child is assessed using motivational activities. One student was able to accurately read entire sentences about his preferred items. If I wrote "Take a brown candy and a blue candy," he got it right every time. But when he was tested, it was reported that he was able to read just a few pre-printed sight words. His reported score didn't match what we had seen over and over again when he was motivated. And reading isn't the only thing that can be measured using observation. By diagnosis, children with autism have social and communication differences. Our chapters on community and language suggest ways to measure these areas using careful observations.

Vague and imprecise observations are not as helpful as specific and precise ones, so push your observers to be as detailed as possible. If there are interfering behaviors, you need to know what they are, when and how often they tend to occur, and not simply that they exist. Every bit of information helps you and future teachers solve the puzzle of how best to support your child.

And—as always—make sure the observer tells you what your child *can* do, not what your child *can't* do. For example, "Did not engage in classwork and stared into space 50 percent of the time" is far less helpful than "Engaged in classwork 50 percent of the time during math calculations and completed 40 percent of the worksheet while the other students completed about 60 percent of the worksheet during the same time period." You always want to know what work was completed and when. You can expand on successes once you have homed in on them. Careful observation that focuses on strengths allows us to look more closely at what engages the student and what alienates them and will lead toward more gains. This may necessitate that the observer be there for longer time periods, during different activities, and at various times of the day, rather than just popping in and out for a brief look. Your child deserves a comprehensive evaluation to develop a meaningful educational plan.

OTHER WAYS TO EVALUATE

If you feel like your child isn't a good testing subject, you can look for other ways to inform the school about their abilities.

For social communication, we recommend gathering language samples. Language samples are generally collected by speech and language pathologists/specialists (SLPs) and should contain enough utterances to get a good idea of a child's communication (at least fifty child utterances). While they can be more time-consuming than a single test, they provide a plethora of information. Ask that at least one language sample be collected while your child is with their peers and another with a familiar adult. We all know that kids interact differently with peers (who aren't very accommodating) than with adults (who usually are), and getting samples in both situations will give you the most well-rounded picture of your child.

If your child shows skills that the school or other tester doesn't see, and testing is under-evaluating them, record a video and have that analyzed. We had one child who was learning to say her first words and could say a few dozen, but the preschool never prompted them, assuming she was nonverbal. Once we showed them some recorded clips of her using words, they began to regularly prompt her, and her word use exploded.

LIST STRENGTHS

As we discussed in chapter 1, "Hidden Strengths," many assessments focus on finding a child's weakness rather than on examining their strengths. A strength-based assessment (SBA) can positively change the mind-set and attitudes of family and professionals.

It matters not only *that* strengths are reported but also *how* strengths are reported.

Consider a report that states, "Logan, at age two, only uses ten words, which is well below the 5th percentile for his age." This may make you feel concerned—and possibly even a bit panicky or depressed. Now consider the same report, instead written from a strength-based perspective: "Logan, age two, has learned to say ten different words, consistently, across all environments. He already demonstrates an ability to acquire expressive verbal words, and the fact that he learned the ten words in a relatively short period of time makes us optimistic that he will continue to acquire additional words and learn to communicate verbally." Doesn't that make you feel better? And it's the same description of the child—it's just that one focuses on the deficit and the other is strength-based.

Another way to make an assessment strength-based is to add in additional information about the family and the environment. For example, consider a report that says, "Oliver is ten years old and scores extremely low in self-help areas. He does not yet dress himself without assistance, does not use a knife or fork, and needs assistance with basic hygiene, including bathing and brushing his teeth. Parents report that he does not have regular chores that he completes around the home." Here's a better version, with filled-in detail and information: "Oliver is ten years old and is improving with his self-help skills. He can independently dress himself, only needing assistance with zippers and small buttons. He uses a spoon, without spilling, to eat. He can remove his clothes and get into the bathtub independently and dry himself but needs some assistance shampooing his hair. He can put toothpaste on his toothbrush but needs assistance brushing his molars. Oliver cleans up his plate after meals and throws away his napkin. His parents work with him regularly and he has shown great progress in these areas." Same child, very different ways of describing him.

On top of being more positive, these SBAs are also more descriptive and can therefore be extremely helpful in understanding the circumstances and conditions where positive behaviors are displayed and developing next steps in the support plan.

Some simple strengths to include in a report are:

- What does the child enjoy doing? What do they play with? What are some favorite activities?

- What household rules, rules of games, and/or school rules is the child able to follow?

- Does the child sit for meals/activities, cleaning up, computer time, etc.?

- When does the child use eye contact, smile, laugh, and engage in other social behaviors?

- What sounds does the child make and how does the child communicate in everyday situations?

- Does the child seek out certain people for assistance? Do they seem more comfortable when certain relatives or friends are around?

- What community resources are available for support and how, specifically, can these resources help the child? How can the child's parents, siblings, extended family, and care providers help with implementing support so that the child is provided with more opportunities to learn faster?

- If the child has problematic or interfering behaviors, are there times or situations when these behaviors are low or absent? Are there individuals with whom the child does not exhibit these behaviors?

- What chores, activities, and self-help areas does the child engage in independently or help with at home?

Pointing out all the various strengths that the examiner may not see and providing information about the child's "assets" give parents and providers a sense of hope, a path for support, and a sense of optimism that, research shows, will improve outcomes.

SUMMARY

Too often, we set up kids with ASD for failure by evaluating them with tests that they're never going to do well on, and then basing projections about their academic abilities and potential on those test results.

We once attended an IEP with a high schooler who was a computer whiz. He could hack into anything. In fact, in elementary school, he hacked into the teacher's computer and made sure that all of his and his friends' grades were As. Our student was definitely smart, but years later, during a high school IEP meeting, the school psychologist reported that he had difficulty copying different complex geometric shapes. He looked visibly distressed, so I passed him a note under the table that said, "I just think you're a bad artist—but you're definitely smart!" His face relaxed. He was a gifted computer prodigy—who cared if he could copy shapes? Too often kids are defined by what they can't do, instead of by what they can do. So, make sure test reporting includes a list of your child's strengths at the start and end of each report. That way, no one can overlook it.

As we've discussed, many factors can influence any individual test score, so try not to get too concerned about a single low one. It probably is an underestimation of your child's true ability. Everyone has strengths, weaknesses, off days, and challenges. Some may be important to address and others may not matter in the long run. Keep things in perspective—especially test scores.

Ask what information the test is meant to provide. If it doesn't seem to be practical, maybe it isn't necessary. If the test information will help inform decisions about treatment and an educational plan for your child, then it may be necessary, but only if you can count on it to give reliable and valid information. If you're not confident that it's doing that, ask the testers to use a different method to assess your child.

Of course, children with ASD aren't the only ones who may struggle with standardized tests. Some children get anxiety about tests, which can negatively affect performance; others may struggle with social interactions and balk at being asked questions by a stranger; others may feel uneasy in an unfamiliar testing environment. For a wide range of students, standardized tests don't tell us much about how they'll learn, how they'll progress, and what topics will fascinate them and bring out their strengths. You know what your child is capable of; don't let an unhelpful test diminish that. Fight to make your child's strengths seen and acknowledged, so your child isn't undervalued.

CHAPTER 3

Communication

THE BRIDGE THAT CONNECTS

You have a child who's capable of brilliance and depth of thought, and it can be frustrating that other people don't see them shine as often as you do. You want your child to be appreciated and to have the opportunity to fulfill their potential. The greatest key to making that happen is communication. Good communication leads to countless positive learning, social, leisure, and employment outcomes for everyone.

Unfortunately, we've found that many programs don't focus on honing communication, and especially social communication, to the degree necessary to guarantee the best outcomes for our children. So, let's discuss the steps you can take to foster your child's ability to connect to the world, and the world with them.

Start Early

Almost all children will start saying words at around a year; some begin as early as ten months and others may start closer to fifteen months. Most children with ASD begin saying words much later;

in fact, it's often the absence of words or a significant delay in using first words that leads many parents to seek help.

As soon as you notice a delay in communication, consult your pediatrician, who can give you a referral to a developmental pediatrician. If you've already talked to your pediatrician and they said, "Wait and see" or "Don't worry yet," and you're still concerned, ask for a referral. If you're getting services from a speech and language specialist, also referred to as a speech and language pathologist (SLP), or other professional, but they're not working on teaching your child to use verbal expressive words, switch to someone who will (much more on that below).

Encouraging and prompting first words as early as possible can make a big difference. Even if your child already has a few words, encouraging them to increase their vocabulary, combine words, and use language for socializing will lead to important gains.

Specialized Support

For most children, learning to communicate verbally comes easily, through everyday interactions with their families. In fact, researchers Todd Risley and Betty Hart showed that the more parents talk to their children in the preschool years, the better their children's vocabularies and language will be, which in turn relates to better academic outcomes. Explaining things to very young children, responding to them, and verbally expanding on anything they attempt to say will allow most kids to soak up language like a sponge.

However, these interactions don't seem to produce the same rapid success for children with ASD, many of whom can and will use verbal words and language, but only when it's explicitly taught and encouraged. The good news? If children with ASD are taught in a motivational way and early on, almost all will be able to communicate with spoken language. And for the small percentage who can't get there, there are some wonderful augmentative and alternative ways to communicate (see the end of this chapter for those).

Start at the Top

Unfortunately, many programs for young children with ASD don't focus on verbal communication but instead on *precursors* to spoken language, such as receptive communication, imitation, joint attention, eye contact, or pointing. While we do often see these skills appear in non-autistic children before they start to communicate verbally, there's no research to suggest that teaching them leads to spontaneous verbal communication for children with ASD. These areas may be important, but they don't have a timeline—a child doesn't need to master them to be able to learn to speak.

On the other hand, for reasons not totally understood, if a child isn't producing any words at all by the age of five, verbal communication is much more difficult to teach. We don't know whether it's a question of an ingrained habit, or if there are critical ages for learning, but the research emphasizes the importance of working on verbal communication at the earliest age possible.

"Top-down" means that instead of teaching the behaviors that would usually fall into place before verbal communication (a "bottom-up" approach), we want to go directly to verbal communication as soon as possible. The traditional approach of teaching language precursors, like eye contact, joint attention, pointing, stacking, and so on, shouldn't replace time that could be spent teaching verbal language, since many of these areas tend to fall into place without being explicitly taught. The sooner you work on teaching verbal expressive words, the better the outcome.

The parents of two-year-old Mirasol had been receiving a popular autism "therapy" program for about a year, which taught them to play and interact with their child, without any focus on verbal learning. During our first session of playing with Mirasol, we started prompting expressive words and she began to utter "Wow!" every time we did something fun. Her parents were amazed: they hadn't heard her talk before and hadn't realized she could. They wondered why none of their previous training had taught them how to prompt her in this simple, effective way. That's a question we get all too often. Why, indeed? And these types of delays in systematically encouraging first words can be harmful since we're usually racing against time.

Many decades ago, it was theorized that after teaching behaviors such as motor imitation, joint attention, or play, spoken communication would naturally emerge without specialized support. We know now that this doesn't happen. We also know that once a child is motivated to use first words, areas like joint attention and imitation *do* develop, often extemporaneously. So don't wait to start encouraging, prompting, and naturally rewarding verbal communication. If you're in a program where verbal communication isn't being addressed, find another program, one that focuses explicitly on using motivational procedures to develop meaningful and useful verbal communication. Too many kids on the autism spectrum are capable of talking and eager to communicate, but they're not even being given the chance to learn how. If language services are implemented correctly with lots of opportunities at a very early age, about 95 percent of young children with ASD will learn to communicate using verbal spoken words. Bring out the best in your child by teaching verbal communication at the earliest age possible and giving them lots of practice. It does take diligence and focus, especially in the beginning, but you're giving them the key to lifelong connection.

It's Never Too Late

Now that we've told you about the importance of starting early with communication support, we want to stress that it's also never too *late* to teach communication. We have been able to teach many children over the age of five, with no words at all, to start talking. In fact, one sixteen-year-old said the first word of his life ("cracker") after just two hours of prompting! A month later he had learned dozens of words, and a year later he was speaking in full sentences to get his needs and wants met. Some children who are nonverbal in the preschool years go on to become very competent communicators.

By the way, definitions of what "nonverbal" even means vary widely. Some studies refer to children with as many as fifty spoken words as "nonverbal." If your child acquires even a few words, and uses them consistently to correctly name a variety of different items, great progress with communication can be made. If your child hasn't had a good, focused program for verbal communication, get started right away with a well-respected provider who can bring out the best communication possible.

Assessing Communication

You want to start off with a good sense of where your child's current language skills stand, and while standardized language testing will provide some information, language samples are more useful. No matter your child's age, a language sample will give invaluable information about their communication in everyday settings, so it's well worth asking for. Every SLP should be able to collect one, and either your insurance company, school district, or state agency should be able to provide this at no cost to you (with the possible exception of an insurance co-payment).

A language sample is collected by writing down verbatim what the child says during a certain time period or until a sufficient number of utterances have been made to accurately evaluate them (some professionals will make a recording in the moment and transcribe it later). Often, the language samples are obtained after asking the child to describe a picture to an adult, but for a child with social challenges, we prefer that a language sample also be collected when they're with a peer, and that the utterances of both communicative partners be recorded. The spontaneity and naturalness of this situation leads to more meaningful information. We worked with a young girl who was a chatterbox with adults, but our language sample revealed that she didn't say a word around her peers. So do make sure you request that additional samples be collected outside of the SLP's office, in real-life settings.

Once the samples are collected, they can be evaluated and scored for the length of utterances, grammatical structures, responsiveness, initiations, language functions, sounds, intelligibility, articulation, and so on. Words, word combinations, and word attempts are transcribed (phonetically if the word is unclear). There are also computerized programs that can analyze the child's language, but these can be expensive, so many SLPs do it by hand.

It's important to make sure that enough utterances are collected. We recently attended an IEP where the SLP based her evaluation on a language sample of five utterances collected in her office without any peer interaction, and determined from this extremely limited sample that the child's language was adequate. This isn't enough. Generally, you want to aim for a collection of between fifty to two hundred utterances to analyze, but if your child doesn't talk much, even twenty-five can be helpful.

If your child has any behaviors that are used in place of verbal communication, data should be reported on those, too. For example, some children who are perfectly capable of using words will take an adult's hand to lead them to any desired item. This needs to be noted. Determining instances where the child is highly motivated and verbal communication could be prompted is important for providing teaching opportunities.

If a child talks more with you than with the SLP, it's perfectly acceptable and desirable for a language sample to be collected with you. Or, if you understand what your child is saying, but others don't, you can repeat what your child says during the sample and that should be recorded. If you have never heard your child use any words at all, a language sample can document how the child communicates (e.g., gestures, hand-pulling, vocalizations, etc.) and will serve as a good baseline.

Once you have your data on how much your child is speaking, how your child is speaking, when your child is speaking, and to whom your child is speaking, you're ready to get started on teaching language.

The Importance of Motivation

No one wants to have an uninteresting, meaningless conversation. If someone is making your child learn words that aren't meaningful to them and that only lead to longer conversations that they didn't want to have in the first place, they won't be motivated to communicate.

Think about your most difficult subject. Is it math? Writing? Chemistry? Now think about someone asking you to immerse yourself in that subject all day long . . . You'd probably do anything to avoid that. Now think about learning chemistry, but instead of having to memorize how the enzyme polyphenol oxidase catalyzes the oxidation of phenolic compounds into highly reactive quinones, your professor has you prepare guacamole (with and without citric acid), a lemon-based cocktail, and a bowl of cut fruit. You're now learning about the *real-life* application of the same scientific concept, but you're enjoying yourself, it all feels relevant (how do we keep leftover fruits from browning?), and you get a good meal at the end! You're having so much fun, you hardly know you're learning. That's how we want children with ASD to feel when they're learning first words—we want them to have so much fun that they're absorbing words without effort.

So, think about the things your child really enjoys and is eager to attain: special foods or toys, activities, even an adult making a silly face that makes them laugh. Using their favorite things will facilitate learning.

Putting This in Action

Prompting language correctly can be simple and natural—and you're probably doing some version of this already.

1. Find something the child really *really* likes. Edible treats are fine, as is access to electronics—the point here is to motivate them, so be open to what they like, not what you want them to have.

2. Next, prompt the child to say the name of the item or activity.

3. Immediately reward the child's word by providing the item or activity. The word doesn't have to be perfect; you can and should reward any attempt to make the word, such as a corresponding sound or, in some cases, any intentful verbalization.

You will have to make an extra effort to look for, identify, and set up these opportunities. And so will everyone else who spends time with your child—babysitters, teachers, specialists, family members . . . *everyone*. It will be some effort at first, but the more opportunities you can find to encourage language with something your child enjoys, the faster your child will learn.

Don't worry about what the first words are, just focus on teaching any words at all. We'd all like our kids' first words to be "Mommy" and/or "Daddy," but kids on the autism spectrum may learn those words later. That's fine: as long as the spoken vocabulary is increasing, we're happy. The more words your child can reliably produce, the faster the subsequent ones will come in, no matter what the first words are.

Here are some real-life examples of teaching language the way we described above, to give you a sense of the kinds of inherent rewards that are all around you and that you can take advantage of to encourage your child to speak:

- Susie loved to go outside more than anything else, so her parents picked "open" as the first word to teach her. They put their hand on the door and modeled the word "open" for her. As soon as Susie made an attempt at saying "open," they opened the door and let her run outside. Susie discovered that words "work" to get you what you want—and that's a connection we want all our kids to make. For various reasons, children (especially little ones) differ in how long it takes to learn their first word, but don't give up—most will eventually get there.

- Manny repetitively turned the light on and off. His mother would place her hand over the switch and model the word "on." Once Manny made a vocalization resembling the word, she'd let him turn the light on and off a few times, then would cover it again, and repeat the prompt. After several days, he began to say the word more clearly and eventually said "on" without a verbal prompt, whenever his mother simply covered the light switch.

- Erin loved to be picked up. Her father modeled the word "up," and when she made an attempt ("uh") at saying the word, he picked her up.

- Sarah loved candy, but her mother wasn't a big fan of giving it to her frequently, so she chose it as a special treat and asked Sarah to request it by name. To her astonishment, Sarah said "candy" perfectly (and her mother rewarded her with it immediately). This was the very first time Sarah had said any word, and she said it with perfect articulation. Although some children on the autism spectrum have difficulties with articulation, many do not, and some even are able to make certain challenging sounds earlier than children without communication delays.

- Omari was crazy about cars, so it wasn't surprising that his first word was "go," which his parents taught him to say just as they were taking off in the car. Then, to expand his vocabulary further, they also taught him to say "car" when they were leaving the house, "open" when they opened the car door, "buckle" to get his seat belt put on, "key" to make the car go, and so on. He liked the car rides so much that he was happy to make an effort to learn the words that led to something so pleasurable.

Be Patient

Don't be discouraged if your child takes a while to learn a first word, or if your child gets frustrated when asked to talk and resorts to early forms of communication, like crying. That happens. Some children will revert to behaviors that have worked in the past to get them what they wanted, like grabbing and even kicking, biting, or scratching. You may feel frustrated if this happens, but it's important to stay consistent and continue to prompt them to use their words. Don't give in to other behaviors: if a child isn't sure what to do and falls to the floor crying, and then gets the desired item, they'll learn that falling and crying succeed at getting them what they want. That is not the connection we're going for here. Your child needs to learn that desirable items and activities can be gained from using words, not by screaming or crying.

The first words are the hardest: language acquisition will speed up as words start to take hold. It all requires a lot of practice, but it's well worth the effort for both you and your child. Your child will do best if teaching is consistent, frequent, and fun.

And remember that you do want to start teaching language as early as possible, so if you're using a program, class, or other kind of support that doesn't focus on verbal communication, or if your providers are spending too much time teaching alternative communication or precursors to verbal communication, find another approach. Quickly.

Essential Components for Success

When teaching first words and early language, we recommend the following:

- OFFER NATURAL REWARDS THAT REALLY MOTIVATE YOUR CHILD. "Natural" means there's a clear and unforced link between the effort and the reward: saying "open" and getting an M&M is not as natural a reward as saying "open" and getting to open the door and go outside.

- WAIT FOR THE CORRECT RESULT, EVEN IF IT TAKES A WHILE. Remember: you prompt, THEY MAKE AN ATTEMPT, then you reward. If the attempt hasn't yet come, and you give up and reward the child anyway, you're confusing them and slowing down their learning rate. Speaking of which . . .

- MAKE IT FUN, NOT PUNISHING. We've had parents who begin by gently prompting the word, but then their patience runs out, so their tone escalates until they sound tense or are even yelling. That's not going to lead to word acquisition. Remember: this may feel hard for you, but it's even harder for your child. If your child isn't getting the idea of what you want right away, just patiently try again. Your child needs to understand that communication is a fun—and useful—part of their daily lives. Prompt in a fun voice, but keep it feeling natural—you want your child to learn to attend to a regular tone of voice. Keep a positive and cheerful attitude while prompting. We're setting up a situation for the child to learn that communication can be fun, helpful, efficient, and effective. Being playful and supportive will help your child get there faster. Your child doesn't even have to know they're "learning"—that can be your secret. All they have to know is that making an attempt at saying the right word is the key that opens the door to all sorts of desirable objects and games.

Some people do decide to switch to an augmentative program for the small percentage of children who are not able to learn to speak, which we highly recommend. However, many people give up too soon or don't provide enough consistent trials to get early communication going, and others use augmentative devices (or no devices) without even trying for verbal communication. Remember: the odds of learning verbal communication decrease with age, so it's important to target this early and intensively. And make sure you give it enough time for your child to understand the connection.

- VARY TASKS. In other words, if you've worked for a while on "open," and your child has gone outside several times, switch to a new and fun word that will be just as rewarding. You'll both enjoy the change, and it will lead to faster gains.

- REWARD ALL COMMUNICATIVE RESPONSES, EVEN IF THEY'RE NOT PERFECT. Some children won't be able to produce a perfectly articulated word at first. That's fine, so long as they're trying. If a child says "ba" instead of "ball," they should be rewarded.

They're trying. Rewarding attempts will help the child understand that they can communicate through vocalizing. It doesn't matter if it's a perfect-sounding word; what's important is that the child makes a good communicative attempt.

- WEAVE LEARNING OPPORTUNITIES THROUGHOUT THE DAY. The best way to learn language—the natural, comfortable, fun, rewarding way—is while you're going through your regular day with your family. Setting aside "teaching time" feels unnatural, can stress both parent and child, and won't lead to as much success. Consider one mother we knew, whose three-year-old child was learning first words. Instead of finding opportunities to prompt language while going about the course of their daily routine, Mom decided to only work on first words for one set-aside session in the evening. Her daughter actually *lost* words she already had been using instead of gaining new ones. Not only was she not getting enough practice, the language no longer felt meaningful when taken out of its natural and useful context. Have your child make an attempt or say a word for anything and everything desirable that comes up during the day. Every opportunity that arises is a step toward improving your child's social communication.

- GET EVERYONE ONBOARD, WORKING TOGETHER, IN EVERY ENVIRONMENT. Five-year-old Adam had a big extended family that included a live-in grandmother, an au pair, and many support providers. Unfortunately, despite everyone's good intentions, there was no coordination of language services, and he failed to progress because Grandma and the au pair hadn't been taught to make him use his words but continued to respond to his nonverbal communication, like whining and crying. Working together will produce faster results. Gains may not be seen in a disjointed program, and conflicting messages can confuse a child.

- STAY THE COURSE. Don't let anyone tell you to shrug off teaching
  verbal communication. It had taken us four challenging days to
  get three-year-old Jose to say his first word, so we were extra
  delighted when he finally came out with it. Now we knew that,
  with enough work, there would be plenty more. But then his
  speech therapist—who had very little experience or training
  with ASD—told his parents that they didn't need to keep
  prompting words, because, she said, "He'll talk when he's ready."
  The parents assumed this was correct and did not maintain
  the prompting we had begun. By the age of six, Jose was still
  completely nonverbal and had developed some significant
  behavior issues (which were clearly linked to an inability to
  communicate). He never did learn to talk.

If these components are used regularly and consistently, most
young children should learn to communicate verbally.

One cautionary note: if anyone tries to tell you that you shouldn't
be asking your child to say words to attain their favorite toys and
activities, run away from that person as fast as you can. You are
helping your child understand the link between words and objects
or activities—and that's the basis of language.

We've seen many children who were nonverbal at two, three,
or four, and who still learned to speak well by the time they were
adults, but that didn't happen without constant support focused on
social communication. The initial work in the early years will serve
as a foundation for bringing out the best in your child.

Fading Off

You don't want to be prompting language forever. Some children
will learn to say the words by themselves (i.e., spontaneously) if
you pause a bit and give them time and space to say them. Other

children with ASD respond well to gestures. (There's a plus side to using gestures: they can later be used to prompt the child if they don't start using the words spontaneously.) If your child is repeating words but depends on you to model each and every one, it's time to start fading (i.e., gradually decreasing the amount of assistance that is provided) so that they understand the power of independent communication.

If your child doesn't say the desired word when you pause with an expectant look, you can use a simple prompting gesture to pair with the word you're teaching. Here are some examples:

- For Jenna, who liked to play outside, we used a turning gesture near the handle while prompting her to say "open" when she was at the door and wanted to play outside. Pretty soon we could just make the turning gesture without having to say the word.

- Adam enjoyed looking at books, so we began partially turning the page as a gestural prompt for him to say "turn." We prompted the word initially and then gradually faded the prompt.

- Liam liked to be swung around and could say "swing" with a verbal prompt, so we switched to prompting him by outstretching our hands as if to pick him up. He was soon able to say the word independently.

Pausing or gesturing before modeling the word will give your child an opportunity to say the word independently, which is, of course, the goal. Too often adults mistake a child's ability to re-peat a word for autonomous speech, so they just keep modeling the words and letting the child parrot them. This can hold a child back, actively slowing down their ability to independently come up with the word. If a child is imitating your words, plan a delay or gesture so that they can learn to use those words independently.

Make Sure the Child Is Using Language in a Meaningful Way

A nine-year-old boy we worked with frequently repeated the last word he heard. If someone asked him, "Do you want eggs or cereal?" he would respond with "Cereal." But if you asked him, "Do you want cereal or eggs?" he would say "Eggs." He wasn't absorbing what was being asked, just echoing the last word (although people who weren't paying close attention often assumed they'd gotten a meaningful response from him). It saved him the trouble of really focusing on the conversation and working to make his needs understood.

When we realized what he was doing, we started asking, "What do you want?" and when he responded with "Want," we began the instruction again, first asking "Do you want to go out?" and once he responded with "Out," we asked, "What do you want to do?" only rewarding him if he responded with "Out." Interspersing the second question taught him to listen more closely, and he soon learned to pay attention to what was actually being said, instead of just repeating the last word. Another helpful strategy with a child who tends to repeat the last word said is to suggest a preferred item before a non-preferred, such as "Do you want carrots [preferred] or broccoli [non-preferred]?" If the child responds with the last word "broccoli," and you hand over the broccoli, they'll learn pretty quickly to listen to the whole sentence.

It's always important to make sure your child is engaged in the conversation instead of mechanically repeating what someone said or staring off into space. Attention is critical for effective communication and for bringing out your child's full potential. As always, using preferred and fun objects and activities is the best way to engage your child. Always give your child some time to respond, even if it takes a little longer than you'd like, because that will foster independent language, as will fading back once they get the idea. Your bright child is likely to rise to the occasion and impress you when given the chance.

Making Sentences

Typically, once children say about fifty words, they begin to combine them. If your child already has a good vocabulary, you can start working on word combinations. For example, if your child enjoys cookies, instead of simply saying "Cookie" when you offer one, you could model "Chocolate cookie" or "More cookies." After a nice two-word combination, it's good to "recast" by modeling back a longer phrase that incorporates the child's original words, such as "I want another chocolate cookie, please" or "I want more cookies," while you're giving that natural reward. This will provide your child with the model of a longer utterance, without withholding a reward for their successful utterance. But remember, using recasting correctly requires that you use the exact same words your child used in the motivational context, with a few additional words added on. While your child is first learning to combine words, you won't have your child repeat the longer sentence—it's just exposure. But once your child is able to use complete sentences, you can ask them to repeat the model to help them learn correct grammar. For example, if your child says, "Mommy, please push swing," you can model, "Mommy, please push *the* swing" and ask them to repeat that.

Similarly, if your child is already combining words into short sentences and says "Turn" while you're reading together, you can prompt the words "Turn the page." Once they've said *that*, you can turn the page while recasting the words into "Turn the page, please."

Make sure to mix up the words—don't always use or ask for the exact same phrasing. We've met plenty of children who were able to say "I want [fill in the blank], please," but made no other multiple-word sentences. This isn't actually combining words, just memorizing one phrase as if it were a single word. Your child needs to be facile with language—which means being able to generate lots of different word combinations. You need to model a wide variety so your child can learn that separate words can be put together in different ways for different meanings, rather than seeing any given phrase as simply a longer word.

Simplify at First, but Not for Too Long

You've probably noticed that when we first start teaching verbal communication, we keep things clear and simple. We always start by modeling single words for the child to repeat and don't add a lot of new words all at once. If you use too many words right away, it can confuse your child. Simple makes sense.

Interestingly, however, there is also some research that shows that if you continue to oversimplify language once your child is able to combine words, it might actually hinder language development. So, when your child gets to the point of stringing many words together, it's best not to leave out the articles. Consider Adam's mother, who always tried to simplify her language by saying, "Mommy open chips" or "Want open door?" Not surprisingly, Adam was omitting all of the articles in his own speech, so we encouraged his mother to add them back into her utterances—and, within a few months, bright little Adam had caught on and had learned to use them. So, keep it simple *initially*, but help your child reach maximal potential by bumping up the complexity as they acquire more and more language. And make sure every professional and helper working with your child is also modeling language correctly for your child at every stage of their language acquisition.

Intelligibility

While many individuals with ASD say their words clearly, a small number are difficult to understand even after they learn words, phrases, and sentences. It's a good idea to identify any patterns of errors that may be present. An SLP can evaluate the phonological (sound) repertoire to see which sounds are present, which ones are missing, and which ones are being substituted with other sounds, as well as to observe in which contexts sounds are being dropped or mispronounced.

Very often, if sounds are simply missing, children will learn them as their language develops—their articulation may be delayed just as their communication has been. With additional practice talking, these kids become clearer without having to directly work on sounds.

Other children are able to produce all of the expected sounds for their age but become less intelligible when they try to combine words into sentences. We can work with these children on producing shorter and clearer utterances. For example, Carly would utter a long string of unintelligible sounds when she wanted something. We prompted her to use short, simple phrases—"May I have the book?" or "Give me the book" or "I want the book, please." After a few months of this prompting, she began using the shorter intelligible sentences, which made a huge difference in her overall ability to communicate socially. Over time she began to use longer sentences, and they remained intelligible.

Occasionally, a child will talk too fast to be understood, losing sounds and syllables in the rush to communicate. It's worth teaching the idea of slowing down and pronouncing words distinctly. Dee spoke in long blurred strings with only one clear final word. Her utterances sounded like "Blah blah blah blah blah blah blah blah juice." Adults would take in the last word and focus on it—"Oh, you want juice?"—instead of teaching her to say her words clearly. Once we started stopping her and prompting a more intelligible phrase before responding, she quickly learned to speak each word clearly.

It can be difficult for children to know when they're not making the sounds they're aiming for (much like when we're learning a foreign language and we're convinced we sound like everyone else, but native speakers can still hear our accent). For these children who don't know that they're difficult to understand, it's helpful to give specific feedback, clarifying that the sound they're making is different from the one they intended to make.

For example, we had a child who said "ba" for almost everything, but once we started to give him a ball (repeating the word "ball") whenever he said "ba," he started to understand that that particular sound had a specific meaning and began coming up with other, more accurate sounds for other wants. Another little guy's mom used to repeat back what he said exactly the way he said it, so if he asked to go to the "Tar" (i.e., car), she would say, "You want the tar?" like she was confused. Interestingly, he could hear the mistake when she said it, and, in trying to correct *her*, would find his way to a more accurate pronunciation. (He had had some speech services on the sound but wasn't using it in his everyday conversation.)

We have published some research on producing the most rapid gains in children who are verbal but have numerous articulation errors. We compared using motivational procedures (see list below), researched in Pivotal Response Treatment (PRT) and described in many chapters in this book, with traditional speech services for sounds. The result? The motivational procedures worked more efficiently.

Motivational procedures for improving articulation include:

- providing natural rewards (the reward occurs as a direct result of the child's action),

- incorporating games, interests, and activities the child already enjoys,

- using task variation rather than drill practice,

- starting with sounds in words rather than drilling the sounds out of context, and

- carefully choosing toys, items, and activities that have a specific target sound.

While the children made progress with both traditional speech services for articulation and with the motivational procedures included, they learned and generalized faster when we used the PRT motivational approach. We also discovered that we didn't need to start at the sound level: we were able to start with full words that contained the sounds we were targeting, which sped up things even more. Additionally, the children exhibited far fewer aggressive behaviors and meltdowns during the PRT program. Your child deserves to learn faster and have fun while learning new sounds.

Here's an example of a PRT motivational teaching opportunity: Jacob struggled with "f" and "v" sounds. We knew that he loved catching and throwing balls, so we named all the balls with kid-friendly "f" and "v" names—e.g., "the foam ball," "the funny ball," "the fat ball," "the very small ball," and so on. When Jacob wanted a ball, he now had to say which one specifically—"I want the funny ball!"—and when he said it correctly, we immediately tossed it to him. An activity he already enjoyed (catching the ball) was the natural consequence of his saying a correctly articulated sound. Fun and easy.

Asking Questions

Teaching your child to initiate questions will make an enormous difference in their ability to communicate. There's a wonderful bonus that kicks in once your child learns to ask questions spontaneously and independently: your child becomes their own teacher, happily learning new words and acquiring new knowledge all on their own.

Once autistic children become verbal, they tend to use their words mostly for requesting items and actions. These words may be used alone, like saying "juice," when a child is thirsty, or in a sentence, like "I want juice" or "I want juice, please." Of course, like all kids, they also become pretty efficient at protesting, and you're likely to hear quite a lot of "No," "I don't like it," "Done," and

"Go away." This is a great start (linguistically), but to bring out the best communication in your child and to improve the long-term outcome, you will need to teach your child the wide variety of additional functions of communication.

One important function is asking questions to gather information. Our kids tend to get a lot of language support focusing on *answering* questions, but too few people work on the essential area of *asking* questions. And asking questions is a crucial part of both language competence and social development.

To give you some background, the first question that emerges in language development, usually within the first batch of words a child says, is "Dis?" or "Dat?"—a simplified form of "What's this?" or "What's that?" This one short syllable is social in nature, leading to frequent and constant exchanges between the child and their caregivers, which in turn leads to a rapid growth in the child's knowledge and vocabulary.

If your child has at least fifty words that they're starting to combine but isn't yet asking questions, it's a good time to start working on that, using motivational components to make sure it's fun and successful. (Please note that question-asking can and should also be taught to otherwise very verbal individuals who aren't asking many questions, using a different methodology, which we'll describe below.)

Here's how you can help your child learn to enjoy initiating an interaction by using questions:

Place a selection of their favorite items in an opaque bag and prompt your child to ask, "What's that?" This may take a few prompts, so try to be patient—remember, your child is used to being *asked* questions, not asking them. Also, don't worry if the pronunciation isn't perfect—so long as it can be understood, that's all that matters.

As soon as your child makes a solid attempt at asking the question, pull something out of the bag, say what it is, then give it to your child. At this point, don't complicate things by asking additional questions, like "What color is it?," "How many?," and so on.

We want to keep it simple and make sure they're enjoying them-selves and mastering this one question. Do this for a while, making sure your child is enjoying the activity by only pulling out stuff they love. Once you feel like they're readily asking the question, hold still for a moment with your hand in the bag, and see if they'll ask the question without your verbal prompt. And of course, if they *do* ask the question spontaneously, enthusiastically pull out the object and label it, with lots of excitement for their success.

Once your child realizes that asking "What's that?" results in their favorite items being pulled out, labeled, and handed over, the frequency should increase. Remember, at this point we're just as-suring that your child is motivated to initiate a question. We don't really care if they already know what the things are called. The next steps will take care of learning the use of questions to gather *new* information.

After they're able to ask "What's that?" without a prompt and have done it several times, you can start adding in items that aren't necessarily among their favorites but are ones that you would like them to learn to label, beginning with every fourth item (desired, desired, desired, neutral). These neutral items can be anything that would be helpful for your child to know the name of, like simple household objects. Slowly fade in an increasing number of neutral items and eventually fade out the opaque bag. Tada! Your child has now learned to ask a first question and how to acquire information. Most likely your child will begin to ask about items in new envi-ronments without prompting. If not, you can backtrack a bit and practice again with highly desired items.

Other questions can be taught using similar motivational com-ponents. To teach "Where is it?," you can show your child a favorite item, then hide it, prompt the question, and then reveal the hiding place. Bonus: when you provide the location ("under the pillow," "behind the toy elephant," "in the cup," etc.), your child will be learn-ing prepositions.

You can work on "Whose is it?" by mixing up your child's favorite items with some of *your* items, then asking, "Whose is it?" and labeling things "yours" or "mine."

Reversing pronouns can be a common and understandable challenge for children on the autism spectrum. For example, if you say, "Do you want water?" they might respond with, "You want water"— not grasping the concept of needing to reverse the pronoun. Practicing with the question, "Whose is it?" both helps your child with another "wh" question while also focusing on correct pronoun use— the child must reverse the pronoun to get the desired item you're holding up.

Personalize the Teaching Opportunities

You're probably getting the idea here: we want your child to learn how to initiate interactions. Once your child has some basic communication for requesting items, think about what's missing grammatically and whether you can teach this through an initiated question. Vocabulary lacking? Teach "What's that?" Trouble with prepositions? Teach "Where is it?" Difficulty with pronoun reversal? Teach "Whose is it?" Give your child the tools to access learning on their own. It will make a huge difference in the long run.

By the way, you can teach "What's happening?" or "What happened?"—obviously, a tricky thing to set up in real life—by prompting those questions while manipulating the tabs of your child's favorite pop-up books. Keep the action going when prompting "What's happening?" and manipulate the tab once or twice and then stop before prompting "What happened?" Then label the action with the appropriate verb, using the "-ing" ending for "what's happening" or the "-ed" ending (or irregular past tense verb) for "what happened." Prompt your child to repeat the verb with the correct ending and give them the opportunity to play with the tab as a natural reward.

Non-Question Initiations

There are other important initiations that can help round out your child's communication. They're not questions, but they *are* more than just requests or demands—they're a way of initiating support or interaction.

One example is "Look!"—a call for attention—which can be taught by encouraging your child to show a favorite item or activity to another person, then prompting them to say "Look!" just before playing with the item or enjoying the activity.

"Help" can be taught by putting a desired item in a tightly secured jar or container, handing it to your child, then, when they can't open it, prompting them to ask for "help" before opening it for them.

Practicing at home, then prompting in everyday, real-life situations as they arise, will encourage your child to use communication in many different ways. And once your child is asking questions or seeking out attention and information, you won't need to be thinking about how every situation can be set up for a learning opportunity. Your child will have the tools to learn on their own.

We want your child to learn to initiate these questions, requests for assistance, and attention-seeking verbalizations, so remember to fade your verbal prompts gradually and systematically once they're able to say them on their own.

The Importance of Initiations

This may all feel like quite a bit of work, but the truth is that once your child masters this (and it usually doesn't take long), their ability to initiate interactions will make your life together a lot easier. They'll be able to acquire information, language, and knowledge in the most natural, fun way possible: by asking people they trust about the world around them.

What's more, studies suggest that children who initiate these types of interactions have better long-term outcomes than those who don't. Our original work with question-asking was with preschoolers, but our team recently published a randomized clinical trial study in the *Journal of Autism and Developmental Disorders* that focused on teaching initiations to older kids. Two groups of children participated, ranging in age from six to eleven. One group was taught various initiations, and the other received standard language lessons (such as answering questions) that didn't include initiations. Our results showed that the children who were specifically taught to initiate not only demonstrated significantly more initiations in their everyday conversation (and we've already discussed how asking questions and making connections brings in more information and social opportunities), but *also* began using longer utterances and received significantly higher scores on their overall use of language. A second study, published in the journal *Social Neuroscience*, showed that the brain changes were significantly larger in the children who were taught initiations, compared with the group that was taught only to respond. You can see how this one skill really keeps on giving.

That's why teaching initiations is so important: it builds on itself, and the more your child initiates, the more they learn, the more they connect, and the more they *want* to initiate. It's one of the best ways we know to help their inner light shine. So, make initiations a priority.

Social Communication

Just about any adult, with or without a diagnosis of autism, will experience social anxiety at some point in their life. We've all been to cocktail parties or events where we feel overwhelmed as it dawns on us that we should try to make conversation with people we don't really know. We often feel like we have no idea how to begin. But the truth is that, over time, we learn a fair number of questions and phrases to pull out whenever we need to interact with new people. Ask anyone who's ever carried a big package onto an elevator, and you'll learn that a solid percentage of co-riders are likely to say some version of "That looks heavy!" That's because there's an acknowledgment in that simple phrase: "I see you, I see what you're doing, I'm interested in you, and I'm aware we're stuck here together for a while so I might as well make it clear I'm friendly." A lot of work for three words, but social conversation is weird that way: sometimes a little goes a long way.

For people with ASD, learning the phrases and questions that help create social connection can make a huge difference in how comfortable they feel out in the world. It may be harder for someone with communication difficulties to come up with the right kind of chitchat on their own, but if they have a stash of learned phrases and questions to draw from, they can start, continue, and even end a conversation gracefully.

Most individuals on the autism spectrum are kind, direct, genuine, and passionate. They make good friends because they care about people, but many report that, while they want friends and intimate relationships, challenges with social communication can get in the way. Marriage counselors will tell you that many relationships break down because of a lack of good communication, and job recruiters will tell you that good communication can help secure and maintain employment. So you can see why being able to communicate social openness and interest is a crucial life skill.

Below are some ways to help improve socialization through effective communication.

ASKING SOCIAL QUESTIONS

Asking questions during a social conversation is a good way to learn about the other person, keep the conversation balanced, and reduce anxiety. It throws the ball back to the other person, so the question asker doesn't have to do all the talking.

For little ones, we like to teach them to ask caring questions, like "Are you okay?" when someone is hurt—it can mean a lot to a friend to feel like their pain is acknowledged. You can practice this by pretending to bump your knee and loudly saying "Ouch!" and then prompting the child to ask, "Are you okay?"

We also like to teach "What happened?," "What's so funny?," "Why are you laughing?," "Are you scared/afraid?," and so on. Learning to use these questions appropriately is complicated, and practicing with flash cards doesn't seem to generalize, so they will most likely need to be prompted in real-life situations for quite a while.

For more verbal individuals, you can also work on eliciting follow-up comments and questions by using leading statements. No one wants to say something like "I had a great weekend" or "I went to the best restaurant last night," and get an indifferent response or no response at all. Good friends show they're listening and want to hear more. You can work on improving that area by teaching a comment followed by a question. For example, if one person says, "I had a great weekend," a good response might be "That's great! What did you do?" If someone says, "I went to the best restaurant last night," a good prompt is "I love going to restaurants! Where did you go?"

All of these responses show that you're taking an interest in your conversational partner, which is a big step toward making a social connection—we all like to feel that the person we're talking to is paying attention and cares. This practice can be a big boost in that direction, and you'll probably find lots of natural opportunities to practice this throughout the day. And who knows? Maybe trying to find these moments will turn you into a better listener, too, and give you more of a boost the next time you find yourself at one of those big cocktail parties!

BANKING QUESTIONS

We have also shown, in a study published in the *Journal of Speech, Language, and Hearing Research*, that practicing with question banks (a group of questions that can be written down and learned) may be helpful, especially for individuals who don't ask questions or ask very few. To do this, we write out a variety of age-appropriate social questions—at least fifty—on index cards. Some examples: "What's up?," "How was your weekend?," "Do you have any plans for the weekend?," "Do you have any tests this week?," "Do you have any sisters and brothers?," and so on. Each question is read and then practiced in a natural manner. For some, it's helpful to follow up to assure that the question asker is listening to the answer—an important part of conversation.

We found that after just four practice sessions with the questions, autistic adolescents and adults who were verbal but asked few or no questions began to use them during conversations. What's more, people we work with report that they enjoy this practice and find that it boosts their comfort in making social conversation, since they have some fallback initiations and questions already on tap.

Alternative and Augmentative Communication (AAC)

We mentioned earlier in the chapter that for those autistic individuals who struggle to communicate verbally, there are alternative methods of communication. Sometimes AAC is used too soon—before the child has had an adequate chance to learn and use verbal spoken words—so make sure you don't rush to it, but only come to it when you feel it's necessary. Consider that any time spent teaching the child to use an augmentative system is time that could be used for prompting verbal communication.

Unfortunately, while consulting, we've noticed that sometimes there's an overreliance on AAC with children who already have some verbal skills and could be encouraged to speak more. One center we visited had all the minimally verbal children using AAC but didn't have any augmentative program for the *non*verbal children. Our suggestion was to prompt words with the minimally verbal— who we already knew were capable of using expressive language— and use AAC for the nonverbal children, who deserved a way to communicate.

Remember that the research shows that these programs don't always lead to expressive word use, so if you decide to use AAC, make sure your child's program is also continuing to prompt for vocalizations. We've seen many children lose newly learned words when the prompting got replaced by alternative forms of communication. Again, almost all children under the age of five can learn to verbally express themselves if motivational components are included and opportunities are provided frequently, and we'd like all kids to have that chance.

Most parents report that they prefer a verbal-only approach early on and want to give spoken communication a fair chance, and that's what we want, too. However, if your child is in the small 5 percent or 10 percent that doesn't learn verbal communication, speech-generating devices can be fantastic. There's no fast and easy rule for deciding when to turn to AAC, so it's up to you and your trusted team to decide when the move might be appropriate. Many SLPs have expertise in AAC and can help you decide if it's the right thing and what type of program would be useful.

If you've given verbal communication a fair chance, but your child still isn't producing words—or words that other people can understand—they deserve the opportunity to communicate their needs and thoughts, and this can be accomplished through other means that don't require verbal language. It can also be helpful to turn to AAC if your child is showing frustration at not being understood. For example, if your child keeps repeating the same brief sound and it's not enough for you to comprehend, you can offer a picture board that they can simply point to.

There are different types of AAC systems, and an SLP can help you decide the best match for your child. Some, often referred to as "unaided," don't require additional materials and tools—think gesturing or signing. In these cases, children will communicate their messages using their own bodies. Other types, often called "aided," depend on additional materials, such as a communication board, picture cards, or a computer.

We worked with a high schooler who had never verbally communicated and, according to the professionals, wasn't able to use pictures to communicate, either. We're not sure if his vision was poor or if it was an attention issue, but when we switched to larger (8-by-10-inch) pictures, he was able to communicate with the pictures without any problem. There are SLPs who specialize in AAC, and finding one that can identify the right AAC system is critical. Sometimes this is through trial and error with a variety of systems.

Again, some children benefit greatly from an AAC device for specificity even when they can say some clear verbal words but not enough to get a specific message across. For example, Dylan said "car" when he wanted to go out, but pointed to pictures on his parents' phone to specify if he wanted to go to McDonald's, the park, the store, or another location—words he didn't know. This reduced his frustration, and once he pointed to the item, we had him repeat and practice the word for future use. Jake could request "eat," but used a board with pictures of various foods to specify what type of food he wanted. Of course, the chosen words were modeled until he was able to use them spontaneously, but the pictures helped him to get his message across when the initial communication was too vague to be understood.

Once again, we urge you to focus on verbal language as early and as often as possible, but if AAC makes sense for your child, work with an experienced and highly trained specialist to figure out the best way possible to implement a system.

SUMMARY

Improving communication can enhance individuals' social lives and help in developing friendships and relationships. Too often communication isn't the central target of support, which is surprising, given that delays in that area are one of the earliest signs of ASD, and social communication challenges can continue long after language has been acquired. If you see your child wandering the perimeter of the playground at recess, sitting alone atop the play structure, or engaging only with adults, make sure that an active social communication program is implemented, with lots of opportunities for peer interaction and regular data collection. You and your child will be delighted by the ensuing interactions, fun, and support that can come from prompting communication with peers using your child's favorite activities and interests. A solid focus on communication will make a big difference for your child in the long run. Also think about the added value of specific areas—for example, teaching your child to ask questions will result in a whole lot of gains in other areas, so that's a good goal to target.

Your child is bright, caring, and creative: it's important to help them find a way to share those things with the world, so they can have a future filled with friendships and connection. Communication is the bridge that allows them to do that, so we urge you to make language a high priority in your daily interactions with your child—and to make sure everyone else who spends time with your child is doing the same.

All the research shows that incorporating those child-friendly, fun, interest-based motivational procedures we've talked about will lead to the greatest success in acquiring verbal skills—and (bonus!) they make learning fun for your child. Time spent together playing the language-based games we describe in this chapter will always be time well spent. There's truly no downside, since you're enjoying time together while encouraging language development.

It's vitally important to focus on language skills as early and as frequently as possible. You know how we're always talking about vicious cycles and sometimes positive cycles? Well, this is another example of both: if a child isn't taught to communicate, they're likely to withdraw socially (or be excluded more often), which cuts down on their opportunities to learn more language and interact with their peers—which will slow down their verbal development. But, happily, there's a much brighter cycle: your child realizes that communicating is rewarding and allows them to connect to their peers and loved ones, which makes them more outgoing, which leads to social opportunities, which leads to more language development.

It's worth doing the work to set that happy cycle in motion.

CHAPTER 4

Tackling Behaviors That Can Dim Your Child's Bright Light

You have a child who you know has exceptional capabilities, who has at times astonished you with their skill and knowledge—abilities you wish other people could see and appreciate. But it can sometimes feel like so much gets in the way of that happening. And nothing gets in the way more than interfering behaviors—that is, behaviors that make it difficult for your child to pursue their goals and shine in every environment.

Babies are born with their own individual temperaments. One infant, put in a crib, will drift easily into a satisfying slumber. Another one, put in the same crib, might scream and cry until picked up again. This isn't necessarily meaningful—a peaceful newborn might well become a stormy toddler, and vice versa—but it can certainly make naptimes more challenging for the second family than for the first one.

While some children may seem "easier" than others during the early years, it's pretty rare to have a child without *any* behavioral issues, especially when you're looking across the board at any and all traits that might occasionally interfere with learning and socializing. Some kids suck their thumbs; some tap their feet; some bite their nails; some play with their hair. Some have trouble calming down and/or need to be in constant motion. Some are clingy, some angry, some solitary, some weepy. And so on.

But because kids on the autism spectrum have social communication differences, they often struggle to communicate their needs. This can lead to intense frustration—and frustration can lead to aggression (and many other behaviors) that interfere with a child's opportunities and participation in everyday settings.

Research suggests that slightly more than half of children and adolescents with ASD will demonstrate some sort of aggression, including hitting, biting, pinching, and kicking. This is far higher than the approximately 5 percent of non-autistic children and adolescents who show similar kinds of aggressive behaviors. Although aggression in ASD does appear to be higher among children who have sleep disorders, health problems, and sensory issues, they are significantly linked to social communication challenges, as we mentioned above.

What do most parents do when their children get to the "terrible twos" and throw tantrums because they want things they don't know how to ask for? They say, "Use your words." But what happens when a child is nonverbal? Or when they have the words but don't fully grasp the social context in which to use them? Or when a bright child knows that the behaviors they've been using—however challenging to others—work to get them what they want?

My nephew Teddy loved trains when he was little and could spend hours creating an elaborate track system with perfectly lined up railroad cars—so perfectly lined up that he would scream if anyone changed their order. During his first week of preschool, he hoarded all the preschool's trains and tracks and refused to share. If another child tried to join in, he would scream until they gave up.

I've said it before, and I'll say it again: Teddy is super smart, and he had figured out how to keep the trains to himself. Screaming worked, so he wasn't about to give it up on his own. But clearly this wasn't a solution that worked for the rest of the class, and it wasn't helping him develop the skills that preschool is all about: how to be social, how to share, and how to play nicely with others.

So, we made a rule: he could only play with trains in a group.

We taught him how to invite other children to play, how to take turns with them, how to make comments during play, and so on. It didn't take this bright little guy long to understand that if he wanted to play with trains—and he definitely did—he had to learn to share and take turns.

But if we hadn't interceded and laid down some rules, he would have continued to scream, since the screaming was getting him what he wanted: lots and lots of solitary train play.

Which leads us to the importance of understanding the ways in which these kinds of interfering behaviors serve a function for your bright child. People scream and throw things because it gets them what they want.

One interesting side note: despite the fact that challenging behaviors are often about communication, an individual's language level doesn't necessarily correlate with levels of aggression: some completely nonverbal individuals are free of challenging behaviors, and others with good communication skills cling to these behaviors. Ultimately, it's not about their abilities, but about what works for them to get what they want from the people around them.

One issue we'll discuss more below is that behaviors such as aggression, meltdowns, and property destruction are all too frequently inadvertently rewarded in school, whenever the children are excused from completing the work and/or sent outside, to the principal's office, or even home. Allowing the child to escape a difficult or non-motivating activity will only increase the very behaviors the teachers are trying to eliminate. If the frequency and intensity of behaviors aren't being reduced or being replaced with appropriate behaviors, they aren't being dealt with properly.

The same thing can happen in non-school settings. We've seen children retain possession of swings at the neighborhood park just by yelling forcefully when other kids approached. Another young boy ruled his household by throwing things when he didn't get his way. (His brilliance shone through, by the way; he hurled only unbreakable items.) When he started doing that, people caved and gave him what he wanted.

It's important to figure out what the desired goal of the behaviors is and to help your child achieve that goal in less disruptive ways. Read on for how to do that, because sometimes the goal and the rewards aren't immediately clear.

Understanding Behavior

When dealing with interfering and challenging behaviors, here are a few things that are important to remember (we'll discuss them more at length later in the chapter).

1. TEACHING APPROPRIATE WAYS TO COMMUNICATE WILL RESULT IN LONG-TERM POSITIVE IMPROVEMENTS IN BEHAVIOR. Individuals need to learn Functionally Equivalent Replacement Behaviors (FERBs), e.g., using their words to ask for something rather than screaming for it.

2. MOST CHALLENGING BEHAVIORS, SUCH AS AGGRESSION AND PROPERTY DESTRUCTION, ONLY EXIST BECAUSE THEY'RE SOMEHOW BEING REWARDED—MAYBE NOT ALL THE TIME OR EVERYWHERE, BUT OFTEN ENOUGH TO MAKE THEM VALUABLE. You need to figure out what that reward is, so you (and everyone else) can stop rewarding the challenging behaviors and start rewarding the positive ones.

3. A COMPREHENSIVE PROGRAM NEEDS TO BE IMPLEMENTED AND COORDINATED ACROSS SETTINGS. Consistency in every environment is crucial for success.

4. **IT'S IMPORTANT NOT TO PANIC WHEN CONFRONTING INTERFERING BEHAVIORS.** It's hard not to react if your child is deeply upset or aggressive, but focus on keeping everyone calm and safe, and start working on reducing the behavior later, when your child isn't agitated and you're able to think clearly.

5. **ADDRESS CHALLENGING BEHAVIORS RIGHT AWAY AND INTENSELY.** These behaviors often lead to social exclusion, and it's not fair to your child to let them continue. You want your child to be welcomed out in the world as the wonderful, intelligent person they are, and not written off by people who are quick to judge. You can't control other people's attitudes, but you can help your child find strategies for staying calm when they're frustrated or in need.

WHAT WORKS . . . AND WHAT DOESN'T

Not too long ago, behaviors deemed inappropriate were punished. The published research in the 1960s and early 1970s provided a plethora of studies showing that aggression, self-injury, property destruction, and even minor transgressions could be greatly reduced or eliminated by negative consequences. These ranged from a loud "No!" to more severe and painful techniques, including water squirted in the face, localized electric shocks, and brisk slaps. These inhumane and demeaning techniques may have caused some behaviors to stop (we all stop what we're doing when we're shocked, hurt, or injured), but what the early research neglected to point out was that there was little to no long-term improvement. The behaviors almost always returned eventually in one way or another. In fact, more current research makes it clear that because most behaviors are communicative, the only way to change them is to teach more efficient ways to communicate.

Which means it's crucial to figure out what the behavior in question is trying to communicate.

So how do we do this?

By being thoughtful and precise.

Each and every time there's a behavior incident, take note of the following and write it down:

- What happened before the behavior?

- What happened after the behavior?

- What time of day did the behavior occur?

- With whom did the behavior occur?

- What appears to have been the reason for the behavior? The most common reasons are:
    to escape a task
    to avoid having to do a task
    to get attention
    to get something desirable
    two or more of the above.

Of course, there are also less common reasons, like a sibling took a toy or a peer is teasing, so write any of those down, too.

Once you've taken down all this information, you're likely to see some patterns emerge, patterns that will inform the approach you take and the replacement behaviors you plan to teach. We'll discuss this at greater length later in the chapter. Just remember it all starts with the data.

One important note: often teachers, parents, and others are already so busy that they feel overwhelmed at the thought of setting up a comprehensive positive behavior support plan and postpone doing it, or even dismiss it as a goal. But the time that it takes to deal with interfering behaviors day after day is ultimately almost always greater than the time it would take to devise and implement a support plan. And of course, everyone—most especially the child—will be better off in the long run with a thoughtful, supportive approach, rather than a reactive in-the-moment one.

Dealing with behaviors day after day is stressful and exhausting for both you and your child. So let's get going on a plan for teaching appropriate ways to communicate.

KEEP IT SIMPLE

The replacement behavior you teach should be quick and simple, something that the child is likely to find just as easy to do as the original behavior—or, ideally, even easier.

Sanil ran out of the classroom to see the airplane every time he heard one fly overhead. His school was located near an airport, so the behavior was pretty frequent. A well-meaning specialist came in to assess the situation and decided that Sanil needed to be taught to find the teacher and ask, "May I go outside to see the airplane, please?"

There were two problems with this "solution." First, the phrase was beyond Sanil's language level, and second, by the time he was able to find a teacher and say the long sentence (which required prompting), the airplane was long gone. Needless to say, he quickly gave up on that frustrating "solution" and continued just running outside.

So we tried a simpler approach. We prompted him to say a short, doable "Out!" when he wanted to see something outside, and, as soon as he did, an adult would accompany him to see the plane. Once he was asking regularly instead of running off, we slowly and gradually reduced the number of times he was taken outside, to teach him to wait. He learned that if we said, "Next time!" he would soon have another opportunity to look at airplanes, and his urgent need to race outside every time decreased.

Sanil was able to use verbal language, but keeping things simple is important with nonverbal children, too. In such cases, we use simple signage. For example, asking a child to put together three separate signs—"I," "want," "break"—may feel laborious. Asking them to simply physically sign "break" is a lot less demanding and they're more likely to get into the habit.

Again, make sure your child is not taxed by the replacement behavior. If the replacement behavior is more difficult to master than the unwanted behavior, it's not likely they'll want to use it. You can always increase the sophistication of the behavior down the road, but your initial focus should be on making the transition easy and satisfying.

PRACTICE, PRACTICE, AND MORE PRACTICE

It is vitally important to prompt and encourage the replacement behavior frequently until it becomes habit. Many people only prompt replacement behaviors when the challenging behavior occurs, and that might inadvertently encourage the behavior you're trying to decrease.

For example, whenever a task got difficult, Mary would try to escape it in a myriad of different ways, including throwing things, hiding under her desk, and shouting. When she engaged in any of these behaviors, an adult would approach her, prompt her to ask for "help," and then provide the needed help. This calmed her down, but it also created an undesirable connection between the initial disruptive behavior and getting the help she wanted. In other words, her mind saw the steps as:

1. Get attention with one of the unwanted behaviors.
2. Be prompted to ask for help.
3. Ask for help.
4. Get help.

So, while she was learning the appropriate behavior, she was also continuing to use an unwanted first step. How do we combat that kind of connection? By not waiting for her to show signs of stress before offering help.

Instead, we taught support staff to approach Mary frequently throughout any assignment and encourage her to ask for help *before* she became overly frustrated. This taught her that she could ask for help without needing to engage in an unwanted behavior first. And after repeated encouragement, she began to ask for help without the adult prompt.

Different children need varying amounts of practice with using a replacement behavior, but they all need enough practice that the replacement behavior becomes comfortable and automatic. It's important to keep practicing during "non-crisis" times, until the child is fluently using the new replacement behavior without first resorting to the unwanted ones. Once you've figured out how your child can appropriately convey needs, ample practice will help them use and retain that new way of communicating.

INSTANT REWARDS

THE REPLACEMENT BEHAVIOR MUST INITIALLY LEAD TO AN IMMEDIATE REWARD. If you've just taught a child to use a replacement behavior, you need to make it valuable. Otherwise, they might feel that the extra effort isn't worth it. Let's go back to our example of Sanil, who would run away to see an airplane. As soon as he learned to say, "Out?" we would say, "Yes, out!" and take him out. To postpone the reward right from the start—"Thank you for asking. You can go out in ten minutes"—would have frustrated him and taught him that the only way to get what he wanted was to go back to just running off. Later, once he had become comfortable using his words to ask to go out, we were gradually able to delay and decrease the reward (we'll talk about this more below).

Remember always to wait until the new replacement behavior is firmly established, and the unwanted behavior is no longer being used, before adding in delays.

Once again, there has to be consistency with teaching replacement behaviors, especially initially when the new behavior is fragile and not yet entrenched. Anyone who is interacting with the child needs to be supporting the new skill.

DELAYING REWARDS

Once you've taught a replacement behavior and the individual is using it comfortably, even without prompting, you can slowly and gradually start to increase the time between the behavior and its reward. This will help them learn to tolerate a delay, which is bound to become unavoidable at some point.

Like many children, Andrew engaged in attention-seeking behaviors when his mother was on the phone. Often her calls were work related, so she was understandably concerned about the constant disruptions. We set up calls with our staff for practice and taught Andrew to ask appropriately and quietly for her attention ("Excuse me, Mom"). His mother responded immediately to this appropriate request for her attention (which, of course, she could do easily in these prearranged calls with our staff). Once Andrew was regularly requesting her attention using the replacement behavior, she would hold up her hand and say, "Wait a bit." She started with just one short second before she gave him her attention, then two, then three, then five, then ten, and so on. Once he figured out that he would absolutely get her attention at some point fairly soon after he asked politely for it, he was able to wait patiently until she was done with a phone call.

Similarly, if Amy's parents didn't scurry to respond to her every request—for food, drinks, desired objects, etc.—she would melt down. It was clear she needed to learn how to cope with real-life delays. Once again, by starting off with a delay of just a second or so before acceding to a demand, and then *gradually* and *slowly* lengthening that delay, her parents were able to teach her to be patient.

Always take your time with increasing these delays—it's worth it in the long run even if it feels slow and laborious initially.

COMBINING APPROACHES FOR GREATER SUCCESS

Figuring out the goal of the behavior and teaching replacement behaviors is the first step, but, by itself, may not be a sufficient solution until and unless you look at the big picture and take a multicomponent approach. There are now dozens of positive behavior support approaches that can help reduce and eliminate unwanted behavior. Read on for some more suggestions.

CLEAR EXPECTATIONS

A sometimes-overlooked source of frustration and anxiety for many children is uncertainty about the length and depth of an activity, homework assignment, or chore. Joey's parents couldn't understand why Joey engaged in unwanted behaviors every time they asked him to get out his math homework; Joey was a bright kid and good at math. Closer inspection revealed that the enormous textbook felt overwhelming to him, especially since he wasn't sure how long he was expected to keep going. Once his parents changed the way they approached homework by specifying exactly how many math problems Joey was expected to complete, his behaviors decreased. He knew he could finish the task and feel good about his skills.

In addition to being clear about expected work, you also want your child to know exactly what positive consequences will arise once it's done. A lot of children who might chafe at being asked to perform a chore will be much more amenable if they know something good will come of it—like going to the park as soon as the load of laundry is put away or free time on the computer after ten math problems are completed. Make sure you're clear about both the task and the positive consequences of completing it.

Your intelligent child wants to know that the work they have to do is meaningful and manageable—we know this, because it's something we *all* want. It can be hard to see the big picture sometimes, so help them feel invested in their own tasks by making them clear-cut and by offering something pleasant to reward them with when they're done.

ENVIRONMENTAL MANIPULATIONS

"Environmental manipulations" is just a fancy way of saying "change what you easily can"; sometimes you can find simple changes in your routine or habits that will lower your child's frustration and eliminate some challenging behaviors.

For example, if a child is repeatedly frustrated because a young sibling is getting into their stuff, find a way for them to play with their belongings where the younger child can't reach them. One child we knew felt overwhelmed whenever his infant brother cried in the car and even resorted to hitting him to get the noise to stop. Fortunately, playing his favorite music through a pair of noise-canceling earphones fixed the situation. Similarly, another child hit his infant sister whenever she banged her spoon on the metal tray. Changing the metal tray to a plastic one eliminated the noise and the stress.

If a student is struggling in class, see if they can sit closer to either the teacher or a helpful peer who's willing to offer support and advice when needed. If they get distracted by people walking by in the hallway and want to run out to see what's going on, try moving their desk farther from that door.

If your child exhibits more interfering behaviors around a specific teacher or therapist, it might be worth investigating whether a different person would suit them better. One aide we knew was so corrective that her student's unwanted behaviors actually *increased* when he was with her. It took a bit of work, but eventually we convinced the school to find a new aide, and the child's behavior improved significantly.

If your child is overly sensitive to loud sounds, you can use systematic desensitization (which we'll explain in chapter 7, "Community Matters") to get them comfortable with the vacuum, blender, or anything else that's interfering with their quality of life.

Many environmental manipulations are easy to implement and make a big difference, but please make sure any change you're trying to make is reasonable, not excessive, and that it doesn't single out your child unnecessarily. You want the changes to feel natural, not forced, and to make everyone's life easier, not harder.

One student we knew was fidgeting and swinging his legs excessively, so his teacher switched him to a smaller chair, which allowed his feet to rest on the floor. Unfortunately, he was mortified at being the only child in the class with a small chair and, without explaining why, started refusing to go to school. Once we finally figured out what the issue was, we gave him back his original chair and implemented a self-management program to reduce the fidgeting. Now that he could sit successfully in the same chair as everyone else, he was happy to return to school. (We'll explain more about self-management below.)

Another student would tip over desks whenever he got frustrated during class, so his parents asked the school to permanently affix every desk in the classroom to the floor. That is *not* the kind of thing we're talking about when we discuss environmental manipulations! You don't want to change the entire world for your kid's sake, just tweak a bit here and there to make sure nothing is making life difficult unnecessarily. Plus, any gains made when the environment is overly controlled are unlikely to generalize: sooner or later, that kid was going to be in a room where the furniture wasn't nailed down. We convinced these parents that a better solution was to teach their son the important lifelong skill of how to use replacement behaviors when he was frustrated, instead of shoving furniture.

PRIMING

Priming is a simple, practical way to assure that your child is engaged and attending by introducing them to something new and potentially challenging ahead of time, to increase their comfort level with it. We stumbled upon this when we were working with a preschool class where several kids had trouble staying still and focused during story time. We discovered that if parents read the same story at home the night before it was read in the classroom, their child was far less likely to exhibit interfering behaviors during circle time and was far more likely to be an attentive, engaged, and active participant. There's a comfort associated with familiarity, and that's what we're taking advantage of here.

We have since demonstrated that priming can be helpful for academics, social interactions, and infrequent activities like field trips. Below are a few examples.

ACADEMICS. We worked with a student who was having trouble focusing during math lessons. We encouraged his parents to go over the math lessons at home ahead of time, and that considerably decreased his off-task and interfering behaviors at school. Not only did he gain the confidence he needed to answer questions in class, but he was also able to help his fellow classmates who were struggling.

SOCIAL INTERACTIONS. Another student, Molly, longed for friends but had a lot of anxiety connected to social interactions. So, in the privacy of her home and our office, we practiced "openers" by going through dozens of questions she could ask her peers, as well as positive comments she could make (e.g., "I like your bracelet!"). Both the questions and the upbeat comments helped her make connections with the kids at school, leading to playdate invitations.

FIELD TRIPS. Field trips can be a challenge for many children because of their uncertainty and unfamiliarity. A class of elementary schoolchildren were going to walk to the nearby fire station on a class field trip, but Alec was terrified of sirens, and his mother was concerned that the field trip would be a disaster. So she called the fire station and arranged for him to meet the firefighters ahead of time. They let him sit in the fire truck and assured him that they would not turn on the siren during the class visit. Amazingly, one of the firefighters also had a son diagnosed with ASD, so he was very aware of potential issues and made a special effort to engage Alec with items that grabbed his attention, like ladders and hoses. This made the actual field trip an enormous success, and Alec's knowledge from the previous day helped him readily answer questions the firefighters posed during the visit. Another student we worked with was sensitive to sounds, which concerned her parents when the school planned a trip to the symphony. Emma often covered her ears and screamed when confronted with loud noises, and her parents were worried that the music could set her off, ruining the experience for her and her classmates, and appearing disrespectful to the musicians. So they took her to a practice session before the field trip. The conductor thoughtfully showed Emma a small sound-attenuated room near the stage and suggested that she be seated near that room so that she could go there if the sounds were upsetting. Her mother also sent her with a pair of earphones that she could wear if the noise bothered her. With these backup plans in place, Emma successfully participated in the field trip—and never even needed either the small room or the headphones.

These various types of priming activities require close home/ school coordination and thus should be written in the IEP, especially if your child is demonstrating frustration behaviors. (See more about writing IEP goals in chapter 5, "Working with Schools to Nurture Your Child's Brilliance.") Becoming familiar with an activity beforehand can head off the likelihood of avoidance and escape behaviors, while creating an opportunity for your child to be more engaged in the activity.

STAYING ON TOP OF SCHEDULES

We all like schedules and predictability, but many people on the spectrum find them especially comforting. While most of us can tolerate an unexpected change in a schedule, someone with ASD might find it overwhelming, which can lead to a meltdown. One way to combat this is to prepare a child for an upcoming change by showing them a new schedule ahead of time (you can use a drawing, or a written agenda for someone who can read). Try to do this as far in advance as possible—you may not always know when there's going to be, say, a fire drill (although you could definitely ask the teacher if it's something they can clue you into), but if there's going to be a holiday party instead of math class the week before winter break, you'll probably know about that way ahead of time, so make sure your child does, too. If your child doesn't enjoy the unexpected, keep surprises to a minimum, and make sure they're made aware ahead of time of any changes in the routine, to eliminate any potential stressed-out reactions.

COGNITIVE BEHAVIORAL THERAPY

Cognitive behavioral therapy (CBT) is an approach that focuses on helping people identify and restructure unhelpful patterns of behavior or thought processes. It is used primarily with verbal individuals, as the general process does require a discussion of the initial problem and an explanation of how to change thinking patterns.

Say you suffer from social anxiety and have gradually become avoidant of social situations. CBT suggests you identify your negative thoughts (e.g., "I don't want to go to the meeting because people won't like what I say") and consciously replace them with positive thoughts ("I know a lot about the topic and will have valuable ideas to contribute, so people will be glad I'm there").

One specific example is Carina, who had extreme anxiety about traffic and would hyperventilate if stuck in it. With practice, first in the clinic and then with prompting in the car, she learned to tell herself, "It's okay if there's a little traffic. I'll turn on my favorite radio station and just listen to that. I'll get home soon enough."

You can do this for yourself, but you can also help a child or student with this, starting with a private discussion of anxiety-provoking scenarios. It's helpful to list them from least to most anxiety-provoking. Then you can figure out together how to reframe their thoughts about these activities, moving gradually up the list. Like everything, this needs practice and prompting (professionals specializing in this area can also guide you through the steps).

For example, Dev had a specific routine he followed each day after school, which included getting his homework finished as soon as he walked in the front door. He sat down immediately and worked diligently until it was completed (a behavior that would elate most parents). Then Dev's mom enrolled him in an after-school club with a group of friendly peers. Unfortunately, the first few classes were a disaster, because—as Dev loudly repeated over and over during the meeting—"This is homework time!" His rigid adherence to his homework schedule prevented him from relaxing and enjoying the club. Dev's psychologist and his mother worked with him on learning that he didn't always have to do homework right away, teaching him to say out loud at home every day after school, "I have plenty of time to do my homework after I enjoy [another activity]" and encouraging him to spend a few minutes doing something he loved to do before sitting down to his homework. Once he was comfortable postponing homework in favor of something fun at home, the same phrase was prompted before club meetings, and soon Dev was able to postpone his homework without anxiety and enjoy the club.

Once your child has mastered alternative ways of thinking about stressful situations that counteract uncomfortable feelings of anxiety, they can try them out in the world, with initial support, if needed, and positive reinforcement for attempting the difficult situations.

CBT can be used in conjunction with other programs. As always, combining different approaches tends to be the most effective way to combat a challenge.

PHYSICAL EXERCISE

Physical exercise has long been shown to decrease interfering repetitive behaviors and some studies have suggested that aggression and other more serious behaviors may also be reduced with regular physical exercise. It has to be vigorous, though. Calmer exercises, like taking a walk around the block or throwing a ball back and forth, do not seem to be as helpful as running or jumping.

Physical exercise doesn't just make someone too tired to act out: research suggests that vigorous exercise stimulates the sympathetic nervous system and leads to changes in the brain's reward systems, so that people who exercise vigorously worry less and have improved cognitive functioning. And for some individuals with autism, it may even improve sleep patterns.

When it comes to reducing interfering behaviors, the benefits of vigorous physical exercise may be short-lived, so make sure your child is engaging in activities on a regular basis throughout the day. As we discuss in chapter 7, "Community Matters," too often children with ASD don't participate in extracurricular sports or other regular team or group physical activities. But knowing how beneficial these can be should inspire you to figure out some ways to incorporate sports and active games into your lives, whether it's with others or just with the family. (And, actually, the whole family will benefit if you do: as we mentioned above, vigorous physical exercise is beneficial for everyone.)

Self-Management: A Vital Part of Any Program

Your child's innate intelligence can be a vital asset in encouraging new behaviors and discouraging ones that might interfere with learning. Sometimes we parents overlook our biggest and best ally in our child's education and development: our child! They're capable of so much if they're enlisted as the pilots of their own journey, rather than being dismissed or commanded by everyone around them. And this is where self-management comes in.

We all learn to self-manage and self-control our behaviors as we grow up. Every time we make a "to-do" list and check off the chores we've finished, we're practicing self-management, even if we don't call it that. Every time we think, *I want to do well at work, so I'm going to finish this project on time*, we're practicing self-control.

Sometimes we develop more elaborate programs for ourselves. A friend of mine felt she was arguing too much at faculty meetings, so she kept track of every minute she managed to refrain from being contradictory. Another friend wanted to lose weight, so he monitored his calorie intake at every meal and kept a daily running total. Tada! Self-management!

When we target a behavior in this way, we become our own teachers: we evaluate and monitor behaviors we would like to increase or decrease and, by doing so, succeed in our goals.

While many of us can launch our own self-management programs, when it comes to kids, we often have to help them get started before letting them take over. These programs help children, adolescents, and adults learn to be self-reliant, since it makes them responsible for their own behavior.

Self-management can be used to help adjust almost any behavior that would benefit from being increased or decreased. We have created many self-management programs to sculpt behaviors, from decreasing aggression to improving verbal responsiveness, with astoundingly successful results. We strongly encourage you to insist that self-management be part of any program your child is involved in.

Here's how to set up a successful self-management program.

1. OBSERVE THE CHILD AND RECORD THE BEHAVIOR. A detailed description taken over a period of time will help you figure out which behaviors you want to increase and which ones you want to decrease. Keeping track of the frequency of the wanted and/or unwanted behaviors will help you determine a starting point designed for success. In other words, if your child is having trouble staying in their seat for longer than two minutes, you wouldn't want to set a goal of staying in their seat for half an hour—that would be way too long to expect them to have success. You want to help them move gradually and comfortably in the right direction, and to do that, you need accurate starting data and reasonable goals.

2. DEVELOP THE SELF-MANAGEMENT SYSTEM. Now that you know the behavior you want to target (increase or decrease) and have an attainable starting point, you must decide the best way for your child to keep track, either by counting the number of times the behavior occurs or the length of time with/without the behavior. Certain behaviors lend themselves to being counted, like having a child raise his hand, ask a question, or clear the dishes: each time the child engages in the desired behavior, that's "one"—and you can set a desired number for them to reach.

Other behaviors, like sitting quietly or refraining from hitting, are better measured by time period—how long a time period the behavior (or absence of the behavior) can be sustained.

There are different ways of keeping track. If it's a question of a number of times, a student can check off boxes on a piece of paper, use a wrist counter, or tally it on a phone. For example, if Peter is trying to increase the number of times he raises his hand during group discussions at school, he can wear a golf counter on his wrist that he presses each time he raises his hand to contribute to the class discussion. But he could just as easily make a mark on a piece of paper or use a phone calculator or other app. Ideally, it's something that a student will enjoy using, so there's pleasure in adding up the numbers.

If you're hoping to encourage a sustained behavior over a period of time, the student will need a timer and recording system. For example, Brendan was at risk for a more restrictive class placement because he loudly and repetitively shouted during class. Reprimands weren't working and, not knowing what else to do, the teacher started throwing him out of the classroom with his aide, just to have some peace and quiet. We spent some time in the classroom observing (step 1) and noted that Brendan shouted out approximately every five minutes. We set up a self-management program for him, using a timer and a sheet of paper: for every four-minute interval of "working nice and quietly," Brendan got to give himself a check. Because the four minutes were shorter than the five minutes he was already capable of, he was quickly able to give himself a lot of checks and feel successful right away. And Kenji, a kindergartner, loved riding around in a toy car during recess but kept slamming it into other cars and even into other students in an attempt to keep the track to himself. This behavior injured and upset the other kids and placed him at risk of losing his inclusive school placement. We developed a self-management program for Kenji, using a repeat chronographic wristwatch with an alarm that rang at preset time intervals, and a small white board to tally points. We went over the rules of "safe driving," keeping them simple ("driving without bumping into other cars or people"), and asked Kenji to try to maintain that "safe driving," beginning with one-minute intervals, which we gradually increased until he could make it through a whole recess without bumping into anything or anyone.

3. DISCRIMINATE. Now that you've done all the preparation and planning, you're ready to launch the actual program. First, you will need to teach your child to discriminate between the wanted and unwanted behaviors. Demonstrate them, and then have your child demonstrate them (obviously excluding anything harmful, like hitting or scratching, which can just be discussed). Make sure the child has a clear understanding of what's expected for the goal behavior.

You always want to frame the behavior positively. For example, instead of saying, "Five minutes of not jumping out of your seat," you would call it "Five minutes of nice sitting." In the examples of Brendan and Kenji above, we used "working nicely" and "safe driving" as our positive goals.

A thorough understanding of the target behavior is critical. Adam was learning to raise his hand rather than just call out in class, but the inclusion specialist was letting him give himself a point when he *first* called out, then covered his mouth, and raised his hand; she wanted to reward him for "trying." As a result, Adam was calling out just as much as before—the only change was that *after* shouting out (and covering his mouth), he would raise his hand. The teacher understandably felt the program wasn't working, but we visited the classroom and realized that the expectation wasn't clear. We tightened it up so that he was allowed to give himself a point only when he raised his hand without shouting out first, and the shouting soon decreased dramatically.

4. **TEACH RECORDING.** Now it's time to have your child practice the target behavior while keeping track (and remember, target behaviors can refer to the *absence* of a behavior, like ten minutes without shouting, which can be worded as "quiet listening"). Again, this is where your initial baseline data are important. If you know the child can display the target behavior already for five minutes, you want to start your first interval at three or four minutes. If they're marking the number of times they'll engage in a target behavior, see what the baseline is for that (maybe they *never* raise their hands) and keep the goal low—in that case, once or twice—before earning a reward. In other words, we want to guarantee success by starting with an interval/number we know they're capable of achieving. The goal is for the student to succeed at the task right away, and for some kids that may mean starting small. One student had a baseline of ten seconds without making distracting noises, so we started his program at five seconds.

Once the child engages in the goal behaviors for the designated time period, prompt them to monitor themselves by marking an *x* in a box on a piece of paper or using their counter or phone. If your child is using an interval system (recording a certain time period) you'll need to make sure a timer is set to indicate the end of the interval and the need to record. iPhones or vibrating watches are great for setting a repeated countdown interval, if that's something your child can have access to.

Recording the success is important, because it requires your child not only to *engage* in the new behavior but also to *evaluate* whether or not the new behavior occurred. In other words, the child is actively learning to self-monitor; therefore, it's critical not to tell them how they did, but to ask them.

Often, it's easiest to start with learning this process in a one-on-one setting, but once the child knows how to proceed, self-management can be programmed into any natural setting with occasional monitoring for accuracy.

5. REWARDS. Your student has checked off ten boxes, which was the goal you set, or maybe they've sustained "good sitting" for the targeted eight 3-minute intervals. What do you do now? Reward them for all that good behavior, of course!

   Have you ever said to yourself something like, *If I get through this entire task, I can treat myself to a hot bath* or *I'll do the dishes and then I can watch TV?* The promise of a reward can help us motor through a tough task. Once we're adults, we can find ways to reward ourselves, but children often need help receiving rewards, especially when they're working on a new, difficult, or trying activity. There are many ways to reward a student who has worked hard to manage their own behavior, and the best rewards are usually ones they pick out for themselves. You want to vary them—the same reward will lose its power if it's repeated too often. If the child is losing interest in their self-management program, ask them which rewards might excite and inspire them.

6. INCREASE THE GOAL SLOWLY AND GRADUALLY. Gradually add to the number of boxes they need to check off or extend the length of time before a box can be checked, so that the child learns to sustain or repeat the desired behavior in greater increments before receiving the reward. But don't go too fast. Be alert for signs that the child might be overwhelmed. If they lose interest in the program or show an increase in the unwanted behavior, you need to shorten the time interval or decrease the number of points needed for a reward. As with any teaching program, the child should feel engaged, positive, successful, and proud.

7. ENCOURAGE SELF-ADMINISTRATION OF THE REWARD WHENEVER POSSIBLE. Obviously, some rewards are going to have to come from an adult, but when children can administer their own

rewards, it increases their independence and investment in the self-management. We worked with one student who liked to listen to music with headphones. There was a station set up in the back of the classroom, and when she reached her goal of a certain number of minutes spent without making noises that distracted the class, she had permission to go back there on her own and listen to a song or two.

8. **FADE OUT.** After the student is successfully sustaining the new behaviors and accurately monitoring themselves, you can begin to fade the program by continuing to require more points or a longer time period before the reward. For some children, you can gradually fade the program altogether.

We initially implemented third-grader Peter's self-management plan at home. He struggled in myriad ways to sit quietly and pay attention. We demonstrated "quiet sitting" and helped him understand what that looked like, then started by asking for just five seconds of quiet sitting before he could check off a box. We were able gradually to increase these intervals to four minutes at home, and felt it was time to implement the same self-management program at school. But after a few months, the teacher reported that the program was too labor intensive and not helpful enough. We discovered that the teacher had kept the time intervals at four minutes, rather than slowly increasing them. Peter should have been up to at least twenty or thirty minutes of good sitting by the time the teacher complained. So, while starting with a short period of time is important initially, it's equally important to gradually raise your expectations of what your very bright child is capable of.

While, for some children, a self-management program can be faded completely—in other words, they'll continue to hit goals without rewards—others may need some type of ongoing program to prevent the behaviors from returning. But fading is possible for most children, and if it's done gradually and systematically, the desired behavior should maintain.

ONE CAVEAT

It's important to note that self-management should not take the place of good teaching. Many children and adolescents act out when they're bored, overwhelmed, or disengaged. While self-management can be helpful in these situations to decrease behaviors immediately, it's critical to take a good look at why these behaviors occur. Often, improving teaching techniques will create a better learning environment for all the students.

Damien was required to keep a daily log in his school journal. He was not a fan of the writing exercise, which resulted in such substantial tantrums that he often ended up in the principal's office. Unfortunately, going to the principal's office functioned as a reward—it got him out of writing in the hated journal—so there was no motivation for him to stop the tantrums. Quite the opposite, in fact.

During a conference with the teacher, Damien's parents noted that he had a collection of postcards that he thumbed through every day after school. His teacher decided to see if he'd be more enthusiastic about daily journaling if he could do it on postcards. She brought some in to give it a try—and it completely changed the exercise for Damien, who got to sort through and pick out his favorite postcard before writing on it. And now that she was thinking about choice, the teacher decided to let all her students pick their own journal topics every day. Suddenly, *everyone* was more enthusiastic about keeping a journal. Simply by being more thoughtful about a class exercise, the teacher was able to cut down substantially on problem behaviors throughout the entire class.

It's important to make sure the activity isn't causing the problem behavior. It's not fair to bore or overwhelm children with unpleasant assignments, and then blame or even punish them for acting up.

NO NEED FOR AN ADULT

A great thing about self-management is that it can take place in the absence of a trained adult. For example, identical twins Mary and Missy rarely responded to questions, despite the fact that they had good communication skills. They just weren't interested, but we wanted them to discover the fun of these kinds of social interactions.

We practiced having them respond to questions and had them add points on a wrist counter every time they did. We made sure to implement the program in places they frequented, like the grocery store, where questions arose such as "Would you like a bag?" and "Do you want paper or plastic?" They wore their wrist counters everywhere and would give themselves points for responding to a question in these everyday settings. This allowed them to engage and be more successful on their own, with no need of a professional or parent there to prompt them. And, of course, we rewarded them immediately when they reached the agreed-upon number of points, until answering questions became a regular part of their repertoires.

SELF-MANAGEMENT AS PART OF A MULTI-PROGRAM APPROACH

Please note that self-management can—and often should—be combined with the other approaches we discussed earlier in this chapter.

For example, we've had children self-manage their own use of a functionally equivalent replacement behavior that we've taught them, recording each time they, say, ask for help instead of having a meltdown. We've also used self-management to rapidly decrease an interfering behavior by monitoring time periods without it while the child is simultaneously learning a replacement behavior.

Jerry was hitting his classmates, and his overwhelmed teacher wanted him out of her regular education class as soon as possible. Obviously, that wasn't an ideal solution for his family. We went to work, and within a day we were able to develop a self-management program for not hitting (we called it "being kind"), since we knew that teaching him a replacement behavior would require way more practice and time. The self-management worked as a quick fix while he was learning how to effectively communicate instead of hitting.

Troubleshooting

Regardless of age, communication skills, or cognitive level, interfering behaviors can get in the way of pleasurable engagement, so we do want to address them.

If a challenging behavior doesn't seem to be going away, ask the following questions:

1. WHAT ARE THE CONSEQUENCES OF THE BEHAVIOR? If a behavior is persistent, it's probably being rewarded sometimes, somewhere, or somehow. Find out where and when this is happening and reverse this harmful pattern immediately.

    Six-year-old Ben got sent home from school whenever he was disruptive. He loved being home, so he quickly figured out exactly which behaviors would get the teachers to phone his mother and ask her to pick him up. It may seem obvious to us, but somehow it hadn't occurred to the school that they were reinforcing the very behaviors that they wanted to reduce.

    Remember: your child is smart and, consciously or not, knows when a behavior benefits them. You have to be smart, too, and figure out what's going on behind the scenes, so the less constructive behaviors stop being effective, and meaningful communication replaces them, to everyone's benefit.

2. IS THE PLAN BEING IMPLEMENTED CONSISTENTLY? If you're the only one implementing a program, progress will be slow or

nonexistent. There needs to be consistency in all of your child's environments.

CJ spent a good part of his school day staring into space, avoiding his work. His mother introduced a timer with a reward system at home so that he'd get his homework completed in a reasonable amount of time. It worked well, but at school he seldom completed his work, which his teacher sent home daily for him to finish. The school staff were fine with his spacing out, since it caused no disruption to the class. Unfortunately, this left the daily burden and bulk of the teaching on his mother, who asked to have him observed. After some discussion of the observation, the school agreed to coordinate their approach with what was happening at home, giving him a specific amount of work, a timed system, and ample rewards for successful engagement. This coordination resulted in an immediate turnaround in his productivity, along with increases in peer engagement, since he was now eager to keep up and work on group projects with them. Consistency—especially with an already effective program—will encourage your child to succeed across settings and with all of the many people who interact with them.

3. **WHEN IS THE BEHAVIOR NOT OCCURRING?** Too often we focus only on the times when the behavior *is* occurring, but it can be just as important to think about the times when it's *not* occurring, because there can be a lot of clues there. For instance:

   DOES THE TIME OF DAY CHANGE THINGS? *Rose never had any challenging behaviors in the morning but started to struggle more in the late afternoon. Once we realized that the end of the day was tough for her, we made accommodations: giving her more frequent breaks and fewer demands in the afternoons helped enormously.*

WHAT ABOUT THE ACTIVITY AND/OR SETTING? *If you know that a child has behavior issues only when transitioning from a desired to a less-desired activity and is fine transitioning from a less-desired to a more desired one, then it's not the idea of a transition that's the problem, but having to stop doing something fun to do something less fun. Think about what you might be able to do in the first minutes to make the less-desired more desirable: a few minutes of playing with a favorite toy or incorporating an interest into the less-desired activity might make a huge difference in the success of the transition.*

IS THE BEHAVIOR MORE PREVALENT WITH ONE PERSON THAN ANOTHER? *One child we worked with had behavior problems when her father tried to teach her a new skill but was fine when her mother taught her. It turned out her mother made learning fun, and as soon as her father switched to her more playful approach, his daughter's behavior problems disappeared.*

All of these improvements sprang from careful observation of when the concerning behaviors were *not* happening. Again, figuring out your child's strengths and successes will be enormously helpful in making a teaching plan successful.

4. IS POOR TEACHING CAUSING THE PROBLEM? As we discussed earlier, learning should be fun, engaging, and rewarding. If your child isn't happy in the classroom, it may be that the teaching approach needs to change. Most teachers will accept constructive advice and positive suggestions for making the curriculum more motivating. Unfortunately we've also met a few who didn't want to expand their bag of tricks to improve their teaching (usually we try to figure this out ahead of time, and if a teacher seems closed off to suggestions, we ask for a different one). It helps to have a friendly and close relationship with your child's teacher—most will welcome more information on a child's specific needs and

interests and will be willing to incorporate them into assignments or to help set up a reward program for work completion. These strategies promote better learning for all students in the class. Please see chapter 5, "Working with Schools to Nurture Your Child's Brilliance," for more on this.

5. IS PUNISHMENT BEING USED? Punishment doesn't work. Well, actually, it *does*, but in such limited and unsavory ways, it's easier just to say it doesn't. The unvarnished truth is that punishment *can* work to diminish unwanted behaviors—but only in the short term. The child may do what's necessary in the moment to avoid the punishment, but they're not learning the valuable replacement behaviors and needed skills for long-term improvement. Nor is any gain likely to be widespread: a child may stop doing one thing so they don't get punished, but they're not actively learning to enjoy engaging and communicating. Plus, punishment is miserable for everyone involved. Stay away from it and make sure anyone who works with your child does, too.

6. IS THIS A UNIQUE SITUATION? All of us just have off days. Maybe your child is having one because they didn't get enough sleep or maybe they're coming down with a cold. Maybe *you* overslept and then you both had to rush, which threw your child off. Put it in context if your child occasionally and infrequently rebels at the same task that hasn't been an issue in the past. Try to figure out what might have precipitated the off day.

These things happen, and if they do, figure out possibilities and give the teacher or provider a heads-up to pull back or lighten up on expectations that day. Don't take this too far by making excuses for every behavior, but if there are occasional rare situations that affect behavior, speak up.

7. IS THERE A CHANCE THIS IS SIMPLY A REPETITIVE BEHAVIOR? Restricted and repetitive behaviors are occasionally

miscategorized as disruptive ones. For instance, Clay had big welts on his wrists from biting himself. On close inspection, we realized that he wasn't biting to get out of anything or because he was being rewarded for it—in fact, he bit himself the most when he was alone and bored. Biting was a repetitive behavior for him. Despite many years of research, we're still not quite sure why repetitive behaviors occur to a higher extent in the autistic population, sometimes in unexpected ways. But if there's a repetitive behavior that doesn't seem to have a communicative function or a reinforcing reward, focus on making sure that the child is engaged and stimulated by enjoyable behaviors that are incompatible with (i.e., can't happen at the same time as) the unwanted one. Clay's mother, for example, found that slap bracelets could replace his biting. Sometimes repetitive behaviors aren't an issue and don't need to be addressed, but if they're interfering with your child's learning or health, it's worth finding a replacement behavior.

Real-life Examples

We know that we've thrown a lot of information at you, so we're including some examples of ways we've helped support families who were struggling with behavioral challenges. We hope that they'll give you some sense of how, with the right combination of observation and implementation, you can figure out what the root cause of an interfering behavior might be and create a positive path toward teaching better ways of communicating.

LOGAN

Logan loved shooting baskets on the playground during recess by himself. He was a bright kid and figured out pretty quickly that if someone tried to join in or got in his way, the fastest and most efficient deterrent was to throw the ball right at their head. And because he was smart, Logan *also* figured out that if he said "Oops, sorry!" right away, it would appear to be an accident and he wouldn't get in trouble.

But a lot of kids were ending up in the nurse's office, so clearly something needed to be done: Logan had to be taught a replacement behavior for communicating "I want this space to myself," one that wasn't violent. We arranged for an adult to accompany him at recess; when someone entered the basketball court, the aide would hold on to the ball so Logan couldn't throw it, while prompting him to say, "Excuse me." She would have him wait for the other student to move out of range before giving him back the ball and letting him shoot it. This repeated practice gave him the opportunity to learn that the replacement behavior of saying "Excuse me" was even more efficient than throwing the ball at someone (and saved him the effort of retrieving the thrown ball). Later, he was taught some games he could play *with* his peers—and his skill at making baskets won him their admiration. In short, once Logan understood that he could communicate the same message through words, the aggression disappeared, and we were able to move his talent to the next level. His love for basketball became an asset instead of a problem.

NICOLE

Swings are always popular, so kids usually figure out a mostly fair system for taking turns. Often, that will include a "countdown," with the understanding that when the countdown ends, the current swinger will jump off and hand over the swing to the counter.

Nicole wasn't a fan of giving up her turn, so whenever she heard another student start to count down, she would scream "Go away!" at the top of her lungs, which was remarkably effective at convincing the other children to go in search of a different swing. This behavior had been accepted by everyone at the school for so many years that by fourth grade she essentially "owned" her own swing on the kindergarten playground, even though she was way past the age when she should have been there.

We weren't happy about this behavior, but when we asked about working to change it, the principal said with a shrug, "You can try, but I assure you, you'll never get her off that swing." We understood his point: Nicole was passionate about swinging, and it was going to take a lot to entice her to give it up without a fight. So we set out to find something else she was passionate about. Her mother supplied the answer: from the time Nicole got home until she went to bed, she watched old movies. She just loved them. Our team developed a game using lines and actors' photos from movies that Nicole already knew and enjoyed. We recruited a group of kids to start playing it near the swing she had monopolized. Nicole was so eager to join the movie game that she hopped right off the swing.

Not only was the game age-appropriate, but, as an expert on the topic, she also was the most valued player.

JARED

Jared was good at math, except for word problems, which he had no patience with. When those came up in the curriculum, he would hide under his desk and yell "Stop!" The school staff would try to coax him out, but his meltdown would escalate until they had to remove him physically from the classroom.

Unfortunately, in their well-intentioned attempt to help him calm down, the staff would then offer him a choice of activities: he could get a "massage," go to the principal's office for stretching activities, or visit the occupational therapist's office for a nice, long swing.

I think we would *all* hide under our desks and scream if it meant we could escape into one of those activities! Jared was wisely taking the quickest path possible to getting something wonderful. With his unacceptable behaviors reinforced by all these lovely rewards, they not surprisingly worsened, and Jared spent less and less time in the classroom actively learning.

We spent some time analyzing the situation and explained to the school staff that the current program was inadvertently encouraging Jared to work hard to get himself removed from the classroom. A far better solution was to change the curriculum to make it more engaging, institute a self-management program that would lead to rewards for sitting quietly—rather than for acting out—and teach him to ask for help when he felt overwhelmed. This one-two-three approach worked wonders, and Jared once again became a full-time member of his classroom.

RIO

Rio was a tall and husky high schooler with fairly good communication skills. He wasn't excessively social, but he was able to understand and speak in sentences. For the most part, his behavior at school was good; however, at home, his parents reported that they felt like they were "walking on eggshells." He had always had meltdowns when he felt overwhelmed, but now that he had grown so big, he had started to break things when he was upset, including several TVs, iPhones, and computers. To contain the damage, his parents found it easiest just not to put any demands on him, so Rio did whatever he wanted at home—which was mostly watching TV, while his family waited on him hand and foot. He didn't lift a finger, which wasn't just hard on the family around him, but wasn't fair to *him*—he was capable of so much more than he was doing.

To reverse this negative cycle, we instructed his mother to ask him to be more active in doing things around the house, but to make sure to start only with actions that would be naturally reinforcing. So, for example, she would say, "Rio, would you get some chips for yourself in the drawer?"—something he was pretty happy to do—and then she would always follow up with "Thank you for listening!"

Once Rio associated his mother's requests with consistently rewarding and positive outcomes, she began gradually adding in a few other requests that weren't so naturally rewarding. But because she had started with enjoyable activities, he was on board and didn't rebel. Bit by bit, he started to participate more in household chores and activities, with none of the interfering behaviors he had shown earlier when he was asked to join in.

JANIE

Four-year-old Janie was limited in her communication but could produce short intelligible phrases. She liked holding her baby brother and watching other children. One day in late September, when her mother picked her up from her inclusive preschool, the teacher mentioned that Janie had pushed another child on the playground. Unfortunately, this wasn't the last such report; more reports started coming in that Janie was being aggressive toward the other students. The school dealt with these behaviors by reprimanding her, then having her apologize.

Upon closer observation, we realized that Janie wasn't trying to act aggressively. She was simply using the behaviors she knew to get her peers' attention. In other words, she wanted to play with them but didn't know how to get started, so she was doing something that felt easy—pushing or hitting—that *did* work to get her playmates' attention. And having her apologize, while a logical step, simply gave her more peer attention and fed into the problem, making the behavior worse.

We implemented a replacement program for Janie, prompting her at school, in the park, and anywhere else she was interacting with peers, to use her words to ask peers to play. We taught her to offer them toys, to take turns, and to join in their play. It took a few months, but the hard work paid off, as Janie gained more friends and readily left the unsuccessful aggressive behaviors behind.

SUMMARY

No one knows your child better than you do. You know how bright they are, and you also know the kinds of things that are likely to upset or destabilize them. It's important that you figure out how to help them deal with anything that might undermine them at home or out in the world.

If you feel like something is a problem, reach out for help right away instead of waiting until the behaviors are overwhelming. Nip every worrisome issue in the bud with the aid of your team and/or family, before it grows into something substantial and leads to changes in school placement or an increase in social difficulties.

Here's the bottom line: almost all behaviors are communicative, and challenging behaviors continue because they are being (often inadvertently) rewarded. They're working for your child, who's smart enough to cling to an action that gets rewards. And if these behaviors have been happening and getting reinforced for a long time, they're going to take some work to get rid of. (If you've ever tried to give up a decades-long bad habit, you'll know what we mean.) But all of our examples have, we hope, shown you how effective a thoughtful, supportive approach can be. This is also true for teaching important behaviors. Your child shouldn't be shortchanged on goals that will help them with learning, socializing, and enjoyment. Our kids are capable; we just need to make activities interesting and enjoyable so that they don't run the other way.

And always remember: your child's intelligence can work for you. With the understanding of behaviors, a commitment to teaching self-management, and respect for their abilities, you can engage your child in a way that will show the world all that they're capable of.

CHAPTER 5

Working with Schools to Nurture Your Child's Brilliance

Every weekday, for the majority of the year, parents take a huge leap of faith and deliver their children into the care and guidance of a teacher or teachers they may have met for the first time only on that first day of school.

There are more than 80 million teachers in the world, most of whom spend a good thirty hours or more a week instructing our children, helping them grow into productive adults. We task our teachers with improving and supporting our children's cognitive and social-emotional development, while also monitoring and shaping their behavior—no small undertaking.

There are around six thousand waking hours in a year—and maybe even more if your child has difficulty sleeping. About one thousand hours of those are spent in school, so the importance of a successful school situation can't be overstated: all children deserve to be stimulated, encouraged, and supported in their classrooms, so that they can grow each and every day.

Increasing Numbers

The number of children diagnosed with autism has greatly increased over the last decade, but there hasn't been a correspondingly high rise in special needs teachers, so there's a higher ratio of students to teachers in special education than there used to be. Despite many educators' dreams of supporting special needs students in small groups with personalized curricula, most dedicated special education teachers don't have the time to give their students the individualized attention they would like. This can make appropriate support especially difficult for bright kids, since teachers may not have the time or skill to identify the incredible gifts that need to be brought out and nurtured.

So How Do We Improve Things for Our Children?

One of the hardest skills for any parent to learn is how to get their child's needs met, without feeling overwhelmed. If you don't make the effort to ask for a coordinated and comprehensive program, they might not get it, but figuring it all out can be time-consuming and challenging.

When you have a child with ASD, you may find yourself spending more time than you anticipated meeting with professionals, securing services, arguing with insurance companies, talking to teachers, checking in with aides, asking for accommodations, and so on, just to ensure that your child is learning and engaged.

All of this can feel challenging, and especially so if you're not naturally disposed to shaking trees and searching out solutions. Some of us are more laid-back than others, and asking for additional help from busy professionals can make anyone uncomfortable. But your child needs you, and you may be surprised at what you're capable of doing with their happiness and progress as your motivation.

The goal is always to be as nice, polite, and respectful to everyone as possible, while still getting your child the services and support they need to blossom and grow. The truth is that everyone wants to help your child progress, improve, and thrive, but people may have different ideas about how to accomplish this, and, frankly, some professionals are simply more skilled, experienced, and competent than others.

Fortunately, there's a lot you can do to ensure that your child's program is bringing out their full potential.

A Bit of History

The first public school was opened nearly four hundred years ago, but it wasn't until 1975—well over three centuries later—that the United States Congress passed the Education for All Handicapped Children Act (Public Law 94-142), which required public schools accepting federal funds to provide a free, appropriate public education for children with physical, developmental, and intellectual differences. Specifically, schools were required to evaluate children, develop an education plan with parent input, provide special education and related services, and create a learning environment that would be as similar as possible to the education of those without physical or cognitive challenges.

This law also stipulated that these children receive an education in the least restrictive environment. This means that children diagnosed with differences should be given the opportunity to learn alongside children who have not been similarly diagnosed (although there isn't a single person alive who doesn't have strengths and weaknesses), or, in other words, "in a regular education setting." Later on, this law was changed to further protect individuals with disabilities and was renamed the Individuals with Disabilities Education Act (IDEA) and included additional safeguards, as well as the guarantee of a free and appropriate public education (FAPE) in the least restrictive environment. These civil rights, begun in the 1960s and 1970s, were a huge gain for all children.

Remember these rights when you're fighting for what your child needs and deserves, but please note that we're just giving you a brief overview. For more specific legal information, please talk to your regional provider.

Starting Down the Special Education Path

When it comes to dealing with schools, the first step is to figure out whether or not your child qualifies for additional support. You're entitled to a multidisciplinary evaluation and, if necessary, support services at no cost to you. Early intervention programs can be incredibly helpful for a young child, so if you have concerns, contact your school district or local state agency as soon as possible to request an evaluation. If your child is under three, teams will often go to your home to observe and evaluate. Your child may be provided with a variety of early intervention services if a speech and language or other type of developmental delay is evident early on, but at age three, they can qualify for an Individualized Education Program (IEP).

Sometimes a pediatrician or a preschool teacher will suggest an evaluation when parents haven't even thought about it yet. This happens more often with a first child, when the parent doesn't have another child with whom to compare developmental milestones, or it might happen when a child is using verbal communication but has difficulties with social communication and socialization— something a teacher might be more aware of than a parent. If testing shows that your child's differences will affect their ability to learn, then it's likely the school will decide that extra services will be beneficial.

Even if your child *doesn't* receive test scores that warrant special education support, you can sometimes get help from a speech and language specialist or psychologist, if you're seeing issues related to socialization, pragmatics, or understanding what, when, and how to say something. Some children find it challenging to use verbal and nonverbal communication in a social way. Prosody—rhythm, pitch, and intonation patterns—is another language area that can benefit from support: if your child is talking in a monotone, or speaking too slowly, too quickly, or in a sing-songy way that interferes with what they're trying to say, they may need extra support. (We address speech and language support in detail in chapter 3, "Communication: The Bridge That Connects.")

These areas may not show up on a standardized test, so request observations: ask the special education staff at your child's school, or in the district if your child is in preschool, to observe your child in natural settings. You can also request that an SLP collect a language sample. Sometimes communication and social issues are only apparent in specific situations, so don't hesitate to suggest settings where you want your child observed.

Individualized Education Programs (IEPs)

If testing or observation leads the special education team to determine that your child is eligible for services, the school will request a meeting to create an IEP for your child—that is, an individualized education program crafted specifically for your child, which includes goals and monitoring.

An IEP is a legally binding document for the school district. Goals (i.e., what you're hoping your child learns to do that year), services, approaches, how frequently your child will be provided with learning opportunities, and amount of time with specialists—*everything* written down in this document—must be implemented by the school. This is a year of your child's life, and a lot can happen in a year to bring out their strengths and abilities, if support is properly designed and implemented.

We'll be discussing IEPs at greater length and in specific detail throughout this chapter; if your child already has an active IEP in place that you're happy with, feel free to skip any of this discussion.

Start by Thinking Deeply About Long-Term Goals

A high school once recommended that a student we were working with be taken off a diploma track and placed in a "skills" class. The parents knew their son had strong academic abilities and were determined to see him graduate with a diploma, but he was struggling with interfering behaviors that the school didn't know how to deal with. It took a lot of work with the school system and a time-consuming search for trained support staff, but the parents held firm to their goal and fought for whatever it might take to make it happen, including extra one-on-one academic support from special education staff during study hall, priming (or pre-practice) of materials during the summer, a lot of teaching at home (where he had no behavior problems), and extra time on tests. The parents' unwavering determination helped their son acquire the knowledge he needed to achieve a diploma, and you can imagine their emotions at his commencement, when he walked across the stage.

Of course, it's important to research what's best for your own unique child thoroughly, before setting your heart on a specific long-term goal. In some cases, receiving that high school diploma might mean no additional support after high school, whereas *not* getting a diploma or taking a few extra years to get one might allow your child to get three or four more years of an education—and maybe that's something they want. So, make sure you're weighing all the variables when setting your goals, and really take into account who your child is and what they want—it doesn't matter what other people's long-term goals are for their children, or what other people think your child is and isn't capable of. Think about what will benefit your child the most and work toward that goal.

Preparing for the IEP

TAKING STOCK BEFORE GOAL SETTING

So, what *does* your child need, in the realm of support, services, and goals, and how do you even begin to figure it out?

The first thing to remember is that *you're* the expert here: you know what makes your child happy, sad, bored, frustrated, and engaged. No one knows better than you what your child is capable of and what support they'll need to succeed.

As always, we're going to ask you to think especially deeply about your child's strengths, which will be crucial for developing programs that will engage them.

We worked with a kindergartner who rarely interacted with his classmates. We discovered that Lorenzo knew and could identify every country's flag. We used flags as the basis for different games, and, as the person who knew the most about them, Lorenzo was who everyone wanted on their team. His social skills blossomed. It was his parents who gave us the clue for how best to support him—they knew that flags could be the key to his social success, because of how much Lorenzo knew about them. Lorenzo is now successfully navigating graduate school.

As we keep saying in this book, parents are more aware than anyone else of how skilled and bright their kid is, and the goal is for you to make that brilliance apparent to everyone who works with your child. Don't let anyone diminish, dismiss, or underserve this person who's capable of so much. If you don't reach for the stars, your child may never fully blossom. It's important to be realistic, but equally important to understand that teaching methods have evolved considerably over the decades and continue to advance. Your child deserves the best that's out there.

MAKE A LIST OF WANTS, NEEDS, SKILLS, AND HOPES

Here are some specific areas to home in on as you're thinking about your child's goals and programs:

1. WHAT ARE YOUR CHILD'S COMMUNICATIVE SKILLS AND NEEDS? Are they learning first words? Is their speech intelligible? What items do they request? Do they have solid verbal skills but no interest in socializing? Believe it or not, research shows that most schools don't provide many deliberate opportunities for using verbal communication, nor do they prompt it frequently, despite social communication challenges being a primary diagnostic characteristic of ASD. You may have to specifically request that these needs be addressed (and frequently) in a school setting, by suggesting what should be prompted and how often. (During recess and other social activities, prompts for communication, such as first words, can, and sometimes should, be provided more than a hundred times an hour!) Asking the school to monitor (collect data) on each time your child is prompted to communicate can increase the opportunities provided (and if the number is too low, give the school ideas for creating additional opportunities). Communication makes a huge difference and can be improved at all ages.

2. WHAT ARE THE ACTIVITIES AND INTERESTS THAT YOUR CHILD ENJOYS? Incorporating child preference and choice into any curriculum will improve learning, enthusiasm, interest, and engagement. Whether your child is in a regular education, special education, or combined classroom, you need to push to have their special interests recognized and incorporated into the curriculum,

whenever possible. We'll talk in more detail about this later.

3. **WHAT WOULD MAKE YOUR CHILD'S LIFE EASIER?** If your child is struggling in any way, you want to work to make things easier on them by pinpointing the issues and seeing what the school can work out to make things go more smoothly. Is your child bothered when other children cry? Does your child bolt to see something that fascinates them outside the classroom? What subjects could use extra support? Which ones are the easiest? All of this gives you information that will lead to a well-developed plan.

4. **WHAT WOULD MAKE YOUR LIFE EASIER?** Are there things that would make your life easier if your child knew how to do them? For example, you might feel less anxiety dropping them off if they showed more comfort communicating and/or socializing; maybe you'd like to take them on an outing and have them show fewer interrupting behaviors; or maybe you're missing out on something—an activity or event—because of your child's communication, behavior, or time constraints. Your first instinct may be to ask, "Is it fair to expect my child to change to make *my* life easier?" but part of being a family member is to support other family members and to work together to have as pleasant a life as possible. Your child is an individual *and* a family member: both those identities deserve respect and nurturing, and, more often than not, any positive changes in either area will help your child in the long run.

5. **WHAT TECHNIQUES HELP YOUR CHILD LEARN?** Some kids love to be cheered on, while others find loud noises upsetting. Timers work really well for some students, who like to know exactly how much longer a lesson will be, and others are distracted and/or stressed by them. Some children like humor; others are baffled

by it. Any and all tidbits and helpful ideas about personality should be added to the list. This information will be incredibly useful for teachers and therapists, who don't know your child as well as you do.

CHECK OUT WHAT THE OTHER KIDS ARE DOING

We don't think all children should be the same. It would be a dull world if people emerged from identical molds. We want your child to be a wonderfully unique individual—and we know you want that, too.

So why do we suggest you look around to see what your child's peers are doing?

Because an awareness of how your child's peers are interacting and communicating in different environments can be helpful in creating reasonable expectations for your child at any stage of their life.

Also, checking out their peers can tell you more about the situation than you might otherwise be aware of. For instance, there have been a number of times when we've visited a classroom to consult about a child with ASD who's been struggling, and then discovered—by observing the peers—that a good majority of the other students were equally unengaged. Many of the classmates would be staring into space, yawning, whispering to a friend, or playing with a pencil. These are all behaviors of unengaged, bored, uninspired students, and became a huge clue into what was setting off our own student's interfering behaviors: dull and pointless lessons.

Finally, looking around at your child's peers may help you recognize what's truly extraordinary about your own kid. You may be astonished by the areas in which they're way out in front of other people their age. It's important to know that, too, because those are the strengths we want to build on.

WHERE YOUR CHILD IS NOW

In order to develop a goal, you need to start with a good baseline. This will tell you your child's current functioning in a goal area. If a reported baseline doesn't feel accurate to you, it may be that the behavior is different across settings. Ask for more data collection or provide your own, if the school's baselines don't seem accurate. Maybe your child is super social with adults but not with peers. Maybe your child has no behavior issues at home doing homework, when you incorporate motivational strategies, but does at school, if motivation isn't considered. Look carefully at the baselines because these are your child's starting points. This is the current level of functioning and from now on, progress will be compared with this baseline.

SKILL DEFICIT VERSUS PERFORMANCE DEFICIT

It's important to understand the difference between a skill deficit and a performance deficit. Sometimes a child hasn't learned a behavior yet—it's not that they *can't* do something, it's just that they haven't learned to do it yet.

For example, Dylan's IEP goals included giving compliments to his peers. This was especially important because he often criticized them. Unfortunately, when he said something hurtful, he would get sent out of the classroom, thus losing valuable classroom time. In an attempt to support the goal of giving compliments, the school staff showed video examples of a variety of hurtful comments that they said children should learn to "keep inside." While well meaning, the lesson served only to provide Dylan with additional phrases that he could use to get a reaction and attention from his peers. Although the goal was to reduce the negative comments by teaching him to get attention in a more positive way, when we practiced at home it was clear that Dylan genuinely didn't know how to develop a compliment. He needed teaching and prompting to learn how to give one. We practiced with different types of compliments, teaching him how to deliver them in a sincere manner, and at the right times.

Dylan had a *skill deficit*—he wasn't capable of giving compliments and needed to learn how to use kind words in a sincere way. If he had known *how* to create compliments but wasn't using them in his natural everyday settings, that would be a *performance deficit* and would have required a different kind of support.

On the other hand, many children may have learned a behavior but don't think to use it when they should. Often this is a generalization issue—the behavior has been established and practiced, but not in natural settings. For example, children often practice appropriate verbal empathetic responses to a *picture* of someone being hurt, but don't use these responses in natural settings when the situation arises in real time. They may need some extra prompting to say "Are you okay?" or "Did you hurt yourself?" on the playground or "Do you need help?" to a peer in the classroom. This is a performance deficit, which can be remedied with the right prompting at the right time. Better yet, you can request that a specialist come into the classroom or onto the playground to provide this kind of teaching and prompting and to coordinate with the teacher, aide, and other staff, so that goals can be prompted often in everyday situations. (See more about "pushing in," later in this chapter.)

When developing a goal, think about whether the behavior you're considering stems from a skill or performance deficit. If it's a performance deficit, teaching in the natural setting is essential; your child doesn't need to spend valuable time practicing in an office. If it's a skill deficit, the target behavior will need to be taught first and then prompted in natural settings, since it isn't being used when it matters.

As we've probably all learned at some point in our lives, knowing how to do something and actually doing it can be two very different things.

ASK FOR TEST RESULTS, PROGRESS REPORTS, AND DRAFT IEPS BEFORE THE IEP

School staff will often give you a draft of their suggestions for IEP goals prior to the IEP meeting. You can then ask to change, add, delete, or edit the goals so that they bring out your child's strengths.

Read through these drafts and also any collected data or descriptions of your child ahead of the meeting. Do they sound like they've captured who your child is? If not, make a list of areas that concern you—good or bad. I had one parent whose autistic child rarely talked but was well behaved at school. The school didn't recommend continuing extra support services, because his testing indicated he had no language issues, but his parents noted that he had great difficulty solving even simple problems, exhibited social anxiety, and engaged in play activities far below his chronological age. They made their case that he still needed support and got the services continued.

Of course, testing can also *over*estimate a child's challenges, especially if interfering behaviors are present. (Please see chapter 2, "The Limits of Conventional Testing," for a more detailed discussion of this fairly common issue.)

A preschooler we worked with tested at or below the 1st percentile on all his tests (meaning that if you lined up one hundred children, he'd be the lowest one of the group), but his parents saw an engaged and smart child at home. He loved cooking and science projects, and used and understood rulers, yardsticks, measuring cups, and tape measures. He also had a huge vocabulary relating to sprinklers and understood in detail how they worked. But none of these skills showed up on the school's standardized assessments. Since an IEP should, ideally, describe all the strengths of your child, it may be up to you to make sure those are in there.

Write down any changes to the evaluation that you would like made. Most school staff are generally cooperative and will make adjustments either at or before the IEP meeting.

What Should the Goals Include?

CULTURAL AND PERSONAL VALUES

You may want to mention any relevant cultural or personal values you have during goal development. Professionals will come up with their suggestions of goals, but if they don't match your cultural, personal, or family values, speak up. You don't need to spend time on goals that aren't likely to be useful.

For example, direct eye contact is often a targeted goal in the United States but is considered inappropriate in some cultures, so some families might not want valuable time spent on increasing it.

We worked with a child whose school wanted to make a goal for him to tie his shoelaces, but his parents were happy with his wearing the slip-ons he preferred.

And of course, we've had families bring up specific and important goals that wouldn't have occurred to us.

Speak up if a goal isn't important to you. Speak up if a goal seems unhelpful for your child. Speak up if a goal doesn't match your family or cultural values. And speak up if there's an important goal for your child that no one else is suggesting. Specialists often have ways to teach core skills that can help with everyday tasks. Children should spend their valuable time on the goals that will make a difference in real life.

CLARITY AND MEASURABILITY

Goals should be clear, measurable, and easy to understand. If you can't count it or time it, it isn't a good goal.

For example, if a goal is "Will improve executive functioning" or "Will interact with peers," that's too vague.

A better goal for the first area would be "Will write down

homework assignments and place papers in files that are color-coded for each subject," and for the second one, "Will engage in play for 90 percent of recess, and will verbally comment, ask questions, or compliment peers at least one time per minute, with prompting."

If a goal seems unclear, is not measurable, or doesn't seem practical, don't include it. Many people discuss "SMART" goals. That means that the goals are Specific, Measurable, Achievable, Relevant, and Time-Bound. SMART goals will help your child progress nicely in a designated time period.

Most special education staff are taught how to write clear goals, but not all. I once saw a social goal written as, "Will know what the other person is thinking." Not only is this goal immeasurable—it's impossible!

Clarity is also important because it allows us to objectively measure the success of IEP goals, which a lack of clarity makes impossible. For example, if we're teaching a child to comment, question, and compliment peers during play, we want to know on a regular basis how many comments, questions, and compliments the child is actually using. Then you can follow up by measuring progress and collecting data on a regular basis throughout the school year (more on that below).

Data Collection Checklist to Include in the IEP

- How often is the goal behavior (activity/comment/etc.) taking place?

- In what setting is it taking place?

- How often are peers doing the same thing?

- Is prompting needed for it to happen?

The schools may offer to collect comprehensive data only once a year before the IEP (which is required), with progress updated on the same schedule as the child's report card, but you can request more frequent "representative probes" in your IEP, and most special education staff will be happy to provide these.

By "representative," we mean what the child is doing most of the time, not only on a particularly good or particularly not-so-good day. "Probes" are short samples of your child's progress. Good teachers and specialists collect regular data, so it shouldn't be a huge shock when you ask for this.

You can request that representative probes be collected weekly, biweekly, or on whatever schedule would be most helpful for you and your child. If your child is engaging in disruptive behaviors that need to be reduced quickly or is learning crucial first words, you may want to request daily probes.

If your child isn't making progress, chat with the specialists about how the program can be changed to be more helpful, and whether you and others can provide some coordination, teaching, and support in different settings.

The school should also be clear about every aspect of the behavior that's being addressed. Does counting each instance make sense, or would a time period provide a more accurate understanding of any progress? For example, I read a school report that suggested a student's interfering meltdowns hadn't decreased at all, but upon closer inspection, it turned out that at the beginning of the year the meltdowns lasted up to thirty minutes, and currently they were lasting less than *one* minute. Although the frequency of meltdowns hadn't changed, the intensity of each one had, and that wasn't being calculated in this data.

Progress needs to be tracked on a regular basis. This doesn't mean that every single response should be recorded if it's going to interfere with learning or stigmatize your child. You just want a logical data collection system that will ensure your child is getting ample opportunities to practice goals and that will help you assess whether a program is effective.

HOW MUCH SUPPORT SHOULD YOU ASK FOR?

The specialists at your child's school have a lot of children to work with and some idea of how much support time each child should receive each week. But nothing is carved in stone, and if you feel your child needs more time and attention, there are creative ways to ask for that.

- You can add to the time your child gets by asking that the special education staff, such as the SLP, psychologist, or other professional who works with your child, train others. Consult sessions for coordination can be included in the IEP.

- You can ask that peers be recruited to support and prompt your child during clubs and other kinds of socializing. Peer-mediated strategies are very effective, and schools have a plethora of eager and enthusiastic peers to choose from. (More on this later in the chapter.)

- You can ask that the SLP train your child's aide to prompt communication in the classroom and out on the yard. Communication shouldn't happen just in the speech room or with the SLP. It needs to happen all day long.

- Similarly, you can ask the SLP to help the classroom teacher learn to recognize opportunities throughout the day for prompting.

- You can ask for more aide time if your child isn't getting enough (or any). Many children who aren't having behavior issues are left on their own, when a little prompting could help them engage more academically or socially.

Your child deserves to have the support they need for a steady upward trend in the acquisition and performance of each and every IEP goal.

REQUEST "PUSH-IN" SERVICES

Too often socialization and communication are taught in a specialized setting, with people your child will never interact with again or, even worse, only with adults. While this kind of focus can be helpful initially for learning a new behavior, it often doesn't generalize if practice isn't provided in your child's natural setting.

You can request "push-in" services at recess, lunch, or any other time your child would benefit from support with socialization. "Push in" simply means the opposite of "pull out," which is common in special education—it means the specialist comes to where the student would naturally be, rather than "pulling" the student away from peers into a special private session. Often specialists pull the students out to work with them in one-on-one settings or in a small group, but these settings are different from everyday ones. They are usually quiet and well-controlled, and skills learned there might not generalize to other settings.

We talked earlier about skill deficits versus performance deficits. Sometimes a child learns a skill but just doesn't perform that skill where it's needed. "Pushing in" to teach and prompt behaviors in the settings where they're expected decreases that problem. You want everyone who works with your child to be prompting them to communicate, interact with peers, and engage in learning goals as frequently as possible, in all of their regular, daily settings.

DEMAND EVIDENCE-BASED SUPPORT

Goals are important to pin down in writing, but so are the approaches used to reach those goals. Goals are the destination, and specific teaching opportunities are the roads you use to get there: you don't want to just start driving randomly—you want your GPS to tell you the safest, fastest, easiest route to get where you're going.

One of the hardest challenges of raising a child is sorting through and evaluating all of the different theories about how to do it. There are many experts (some self-proclaimed) who want to tell you what you're doing wrong and how to fix your parenting mistakes.

When you have a child with any kind of difference, you're likely to seek out advice and information on the best way to support them. Some theories and approaches can even be harmful, like certain extreme diets and specific medications that result in long-term negative consequences.

How do you find good information and services without putting yourself at risk of being led astray? The most important thing you can do is to make sure that any information or help you get, whether it's for support, medical care, or teaching, is evidence-based. This means that there are research studies to back up the procedure, and these studies have been conducted in multiple research settings, with replicable positive results. If a procedure can't be replicated by other researchers, it's not worth pursuing.

Unfortunately, there are people who will reassure you that their approach *is* evidence-based even if it's not true. The good news is that you can google an approach or program on your own: if it really *is* evidenced-based, you'll see a list of "scholarly articles for X." If you can't find any, the procedure lacks evidence. Make sure the scholarly articles you read appear in a peer-reviewed journal (you can google this, too), which tells you that other experts in the field have reviewed and critiqued the research. If you search for a systematic analysis, meta-analysis, or review article about any approach you're considering before plunging in, and read up on it, you will be making sure your child is getting effective support.

And if your research tells you that something has mixed outcomes or can be ineffective or harmful for a child, please feel free to question anyone's decision to use that method and feel even freer to say "No thanks" to a program that isn't evidence-based or just doesn't feel right. Your child doesn't have time for ineffective—or worse, negatively impacting—approaches.

DON'T FORGET RECESS

Children with ASD often struggle to engage socially with their peers, which makes recess an incredibly important part of the day for them: it's as much (if not more) of a learning experience for kids with social challenges as any classroom instruction. So it's crucial that they be supported with trained providers during that time. Even when all other areas are at expected levels, social challenges tend to linger through adulthood, so it's clear they're an important area to target, but many of the playground staff or aides that attend to the child during recess are the least educated of the school staff.

Although some SLPs and teachers with advanced degrees will "push in" to the child's natural environment during recess or lunch, some schools don't do this, for a variety of stated reasons. However, too often an observer will discover that the students are getting little to no support during unstructured times with their peers.

One excuse for that is the often heard "It's recess! Every child gets to pick what they want to do during recess—so if a student chooses to be alone the entire time, we let them!" Transfer that argument to an academic area, and you'll see how ridiculous it is: after all, if every child got to pick which book they wanted to read, and a student chose not to read *any* book, most teachers would be concerned. But sometimes those same teachers and special ed administrators will shrug off socialization, which is so critical for every child and such an enormous part of what can be absorbed and gained in a school setting.

Verbal adolescents and adults tell us that they yearn for friends. If the school feels your child needs "down time," let them know that you will make sure you provide them with that at home, not during school hours, when valuable friendships can be formed. Letting them wander the playground alone without support may be setting them up for a lifetime of loneliness, depression, and anxiety about their ability to navigate social situations.

ASK FOR A PEER MEDIATION PROGRAM

There may never be enough adults to go around, so peers are a great resource—all the more so because, in many situations, it's actually more appropriate for a peer to provide assistance. From preschool through adulthood, you can always find willing and capable peers to recruit for extra support.

Peer mediation is something that should be added to an IEP for any children experiencing social challenges, but programs need to be set up thoughtfully, systematically, and with the right kids. For academic support, enlisting one peer is great, but for socializing outside of the classroom, the research promotes selecting a peer clique or a group of peers.

We've selected peers in several ways. Sometimes we do it ourselves, starting with a small presentation and discussion: we talk to a class about how people have circles of friends and how it would feel not to have any (or many), and ways that you can reach out to help someone who might be in need of friendship. After the presentation, we hand out a piece of paper to each student that says, "I would like to help out now" or "I would like to help out later." (We deliberately omit any statement indicating "I don't want to help," because the lack of support to someone in need is not a good option.)

Some teachers are comfortable picking out peers who will be

supportive, kind, and effective, but others need specific suggestions and guidance. If the teacher has never arranged a peer-mediated program, it may be useful to ask for assistance from special education staff who are experienced with the procedures.

No matter the students' age, academic, or communication level, we've never had a challenge recruiting competent and willing peers. The truth is that most kids like to be helpers.

Once the peers have been selected, the person in charge will have to remember that the peers are now support "staff." They need to be taught, provided with feedback, and praised for their good efforts.

If they're very young, they may need to be shown what to do, as well as told. For example, if a preschooler is learning first words, we show the volunteering classmates how to select a motivating object, wait for a word, then give it to the child after an attempt or a good word. If it's a more verbal student who needs support with socializing, we suggest inviting the student to play, asking them questions, and prompting responses. For our teens and young adults who need extra support on academics, we recruit classmates to study after school with them. With all ages, we sometimes use role-playing initially.

The literature is full of great examples of peer mediation. Here are some things we've seen peers do in and out of the classroom to help support a student with ASD:

- reminding the student to finish their work or transition when off task,

- ignoring interfering behavior, while praising and responding to appropriate engagement and behavior,

- responding to questions or prompting questions,

- teaching turn-taking and playing games,

- teaching sightreading,

- further explaining a teacher's directions,

- providing feedback on academic work, and

- teaching new vocabulary words and prompting longer utterances.

Peer-mediated support often results in happy bonuses, such as playdates, invitations to events, and social and emotional connection outside of the designated peer mediation program. Getting peers to assist with and support your child's needs gives them the opportunity to experience how enjoyable your child's company is and how much fun they can have together. The literature is full of examples of effective peer mediation programs, so just about any area that your child could use support in can be encouraged with a good, carefully planned peer-mediated program.

Please see chapter 7, "Community Matters," for details about using peer-mediated interventions (PMI) specifically to improve a child's social skills.

INCLUDE SMALL REQUESTS

Include in your IEP requests and goals that may seem small, like using your child's favorite activities and items during specialists' sessions or ensuring that enough opportunities for social interaction with peers are provided. If they're included, they'll happen. If they're not, they might not.

Finally, make sure you ask for regular meetings throughout the year to evaluate how everything is going, aiming for once a month (see more on what you should be looking for at those meetings in the section below).

A FEW QUESTIONS TO ASK AT YOUR ANNUAL IEP MEETING FOR SETTING THE UPCOMING YEAR'S GOALS:

- Is a peer-mediated program going to be implemented to help support social goals?

- Is self-management going to be used to help your child stay on task and complete assignments?

- What specific motivational components are going to be incorporated into the curriculum to make sure your child's interests are captured?

- What specific vocabulary words, language goals, and linguistic concepts are going to be targeted, so you can prompt them as they arise at home and in other settings for faster learning?

- What prompting is going to be used and how is it going to be reduced to create independence?

- Will multicomponent programs be implemented across all settings?

- What type of home-school coordination will be in place to assure that everyone is focusing on the same behaviors in a seamless and consistent manner?

BRING ALL YOUR PLAYERS TO THE MEETING

If possible, we recommend that you bring at least one other person who knows your child well to the IEP meeting with you. This can be a spouse, relative, specialist, or anyone else you trust, who appreciates how brilliant and unique your child is. It can be difficult hearing your child's weaknesses detailed, and having someone you rely on at your side can help you both emotionally and in making the arguments you might need to get the right kind of support lined up.

If you can't arrange for someone to come with you, ask to be sent the IEP goals and progress report ahead of time (something we recommend anyway) so you can go over it with someone you trust, and then request the adjustments you discussed with them once you're at the meeting.

Alternatively, you can wait to sign the document until after the IEP meeting is over and you've brought the plan home with you, discussed it with someone you trust, and adjusted any goals or benchmarks that don't feel right to you.

Many people have friends or acquaintances who also have children receiving special education services and who can support and advise them during the IEP process. There are also many online resources that can help you figure out if goals are clear and measurable, and, if they're not, what steps you can take to change that.

In addition to having someone who knows your goals and can support you emotionally, it's helpful to also have a "quarterback"— that is, someone who can help oversee the big picture and step in to direct the process when necessary. This should also be someone you trust, with knowledge and experience in the autism field, like an autism expert at a university, a retired specialist, a past or current provider who sees your child outside of the school, or a friend or family member who has experience in special education.

Generally, this support person is someone who can be objective, who understands what can and can't be accomplished, and who will support you on an ongoing basis. Sometimes stressful issues come up, and you need an outside opinion. Having this person in your life can make a huge difference. Make sure this person will be able to respond rapidly by email, text, or phone in an emergency situation.

Some families, with the means to do so, will choose a professional paid advocate, who can help them fight for their rights if they're not getting what they need out of the school system. This is not a necessity, by any means, so don't worry if you can't afford to do this. Being thoughtful and involved yourself is far more important than bringing in a paid outsider. Some people even go so far as to hire an attorney to represent their interests with a school, but their services are expensive, and administrators may feel intimidated and coerced by the presence of an attorney, so we only recommend this in extreme cases, and even then only if it's not going to overwhelm a family financially.

If you do have the means and desire to hire a professional, you want to trust that their fees are reasonable and they're not gouging you—we've sadly seen some bill high prices for their services and then stretch out meetings well after decisions have been made, just for the extra billable hours. If you're finding that's happening, look for someone else.

Make sure your values and goals align with those of your chosen quarterback, whether they're a friend or for-hire. You'll want them to be able to give you advice when you're confused, help you convey what you want to the school, support you should issues arise, and rejoice in your child's successes.

Also—and we can't stress this enough—you want someone who advocates firmly but *nicely*. If someone is your representative or ally at meetings, you want them to be respectful, polite, and determined. If they alienate staff by being rude or impatient, you might lose other potential allies. At the same time, they should be willing to hold firm to goals that are important to you and your child.

Most importantly, your quarterback should push to make sure the goals of the IEP are implemented appropriately and effectively. Too many parents leave an IEP meeting feeling confused, uncertain about the future, and/or anxious that their child isn't going to get the support they were hoping for. A quarterback with real expertise can help you sift through the paperwork, make suggestions, and support you.

Most educators do want the best for your child, but some have more administrative experience than special education experience and may need guidance from a person knowledgeable in ASD. Seek out help from individuals you trust who are familiar with the process and the literature. Everyone will benefit.

If you generally feel good (or at least *better*) after a meeting, phone call, text, or email with your quarterback, you've found the right person.

PUSH IF NECESSARY

There are times to push hard for what your child needs. For example, if your child needs support at lunch for socialization, and the school's first response is to say that no one is available then, push the issue—insist on their finding someone. If your child needs a one-on-one to succeed in the classroom, ask for that.

Wait to sign the IEP until you're completely satisfied with it. Once it's signed, while small things can often be changed with a meeting or chat with the specialist or teacher, it can be more difficult and time-consuming to make changes in bigger decisions like placement, services, and the number of minutes of services provided. (Note: most states require a signed IEP, but a few do not.)

The IEP is a collaborative document. Parent input is important. Read the parent rights form that you should receive prior to each IEP meeting so that you understand your power and rights. Schools are accustomed to parents taking a few days to study the IEP document, so take time and ask for changes, additions, or deletions if something doesn't feel right or needs adjusting. Don't rush to agree with the IEP because you feel pressured to in any way.

If you just can't come to an agreement with the school, you can file for a due process hearing, where an impartial officer will hear both sides of the dispute. This process is time-consuming, expensive, and stressful. It's preferable to work with your school to get the goals and program right. Also, understand that if you're asking for a change in placement, such as moving from special education to regular education or vice versa, and that gets disputed, the child will "stay put" (this is sometimes called "pendency") in their current program until the dispute is resolved. For this reason, efficient, timely resolution of issues is desirable.

Ask for what your child needs and let the school figure out where they will get the needed support. There are so many options, ranging from a change in services at the school to enrollment in a completely different setting. Schools will usually work with you to determine how and where your child will make the most progress, but you need to make your voice heard.

JOSHUA'S STORY

We've thrown a lot at you here, and sometimes it's easiest to see the advice in action. Here's the story of Joshua, which gives you a good sense of how important and life-changing a good IEP can be.

Joshua was only in kindergarten, but he was bilingual and could read fluently—he carted around a college anatomy book, which, in his words, had "a wealth of information." He also loved to study the periodic table and geography and knew extensive, detailed facts about both subjects. He taught himself math and was already doing eighth-grade algebra.

There was no question that Joshua was a brilliant kid, so we were shocked when his report card painted a picture of a kid who was struggling in almost every subject. His concerned parents agreed we should meet with the school staff.

His busy teachers seemed unaware of his innate brilliance, so they ascribed his lack of interest and attention in class to an inability to concentrate, rather than to boredom, which we realized fairly quickly was the case.

So, at our meeting with the school staff, we focused on figuring out ways to challenge him more academically, while actively supporting him in the areas he struggled with, like social communication. We all agreed on the following goals:

- ACADEMICS. Joshua is advanced academically in all areas. The teacher will test him individually in the near future and provide feedback.

  In order to challenge him, the school will consider: (1) placing him in academic classes that are a higher grade; (2) grouping him with another student in his class with high skills; (3) providing (homework) assignments that are at his academic level.

- SOCIAL. To improve socialization with peers (he reports that he wants to make friends and play with his classmates), (1) Joshua will participate in an after-school group from 4:00 p.m. to 5:00 p.m.; (2) the school will create clubs, such as math club, with peers, to encourage socialization around his strengths/ favorite activities; (3) the school counselor will have him participate with one or two other students in a social group and will prompt him to initiate play, join play, and engage with peers at recesses.

- CLASS PARTICIPATION. (1) The teacher will prompt Joshua to use a verbal response, such as "I'm not sure," "I don't know," and "Can you ask me later?," as replacements for not responding. (2) On Fridays, the teacher will provide the parents with general themes for the upcoming week, so they can go over topics that may be more challenging for him to answer during group discussion. (3) If he's still struggling, the teacher will work with him one-on-one to encourage responding and then will gradually add in other students until he is comfortable talking in front of the class.

- OBSERVATIONS. The teacher will arrange periodic observations during recess to assess and target his socialization, looking for activities that he enjoys.

- PRIMING. Because Joshua has difficulties socially interacting and responding in group situations, the family will practice activities (sharing, answering questions, etc.) at home to prepare him and help his confidence.

- HOME/SCHOOL COORDINATION. The teacher will inform the family of his use of any new procedures, and if she notices areas that cause excessive challenges for him, so that his team can develop a plan for targeting them. The teacher will let the family know of other students that he gets along with so they can plan playdates after school and on the weekends.

- REGROUP. We will meet again in a month to discuss his progress/needs.

Once we had specific, detailed, individualized support in place for Joshua, his amazing—and now fully aware and on-board—teachers were able to support him in a way that brought out his strengths. This multicomponent plan resulted in a successful year, and his teachers learned to recognize the function of his interrupting behaviors and adapt things so that he could learn and enjoy school. The only issue that remained was that he was so far ahead in math that his teachers couldn't keep up with him, and he needed to switch to online math lessons!

Once You Have Your IEP

Once you have your child's IEP in place, make sure each and every person your child interacts with knows and understands its goals, by writing out a simplified overview and giving it to each person. It can be hard to read a legal document, so an easy-to-read list will be a boon to busy teachers and specialists.

Have regular, friendly contact with your child's teacher, aide, and support staff, to whatever extent other commitments permit. If you have the time and opportunity, think about volunteering in the classroom or stopping by the school occasionally. Similarly, if it's an option for you, see if you can drop off or pick up your child from school as often as possible, and try to touch base with the teacher while you're there. If you can't show up at school regularly (and many parents can't, for a variety of understandable reasons), keep a back-and-forth email chain going with the teacher, specialist, and/or aide, or ask that a daily log be sent back and forth. (Actually, a log is a good idea even if you *do* have regular contact with the teacher and school staff.) In this log, make sure that data is reported. General notes like "It was a good day" are less helpful than specific ones like "Suzie approached Mindy during art and spontaneously asked her for the crayons," or "With prompting, TJ used two-word combinations twenty times. Five were responses to peers." Specifics are enormously helpful.

Most teachers and specialists have a large bag of tricks, so try to acquaint yourself with their recommendations. Sift through the ideas, try them, and get back to the school about what works at home, so you can coordinate approaches.

Information has to flow both ways: you need to report any progress you're seeing at home, so people at school know to expect and encourage those gains.

Many studies show that autistic individuals learn faster and are more likely to maintain their gains if programs are seamlessly coordinated across settings. That means everyone should be on the same page and working toward the same goals, at home, at school, and in any other environment.

Coordination is crucial for fast and long-lasting gains. If something works, spread the word.

CHEAT SHEET

Similar to the simplified IEP goal list, we also recommend creating a "cheat sheet"—a short list of the most important things you want people to know about your child: their likes and dislikes, their immediate and long-term goals, their areas of strength and weakness. It's something you can instantly share with anyone who might be interacting with or instructing them.

For example, one student's cheat sheet listed as goals "Engaging in academic assignments," "Interacting with peers," and "Using the past tense." It also included the fact that he reacted negatively to reprimands but responded well to praise or a cheerful "Let's try again!" These little helpful tips can really make a difference for your child. Try to list them with bullet points to keep them as short and simple as possible. We want them to be read often as a quick reminder, and busy people don't want to have to wade through extraneous information to get to the important stuff.

Often the school doesn't know your child's special interests or greatest strengths unless you point them out and continue to stress them. I know we keep saying this, but it's so key to success that it bears repeating.

Nick, a fifth grader, was a strong reader but preferred to read books written for younger children. When the parents mentioned this to the teacher, she had him go to the kindergarten class once a week to read to the younger students. This was a great example of using an interest in an appropriate, skill-building, and social way.

THE REGULAR MEETINGS YOU REQUESTED IN THE IEP

Team meetings are usually held at lunch or after school (ideally monthly, or at least quarterly during the parent/teacher conference and report card release), often in the child's classroom or in a special education room, and should include, at minimum, the teacher, any individual who's overseeing your child's program (at many schools this is a program specialist who provides training, consultation, and sometimes direct services to your child), and your quarterback. Ask if the specialists who regularly see your child (SLP, OT) can attend the meeting, and, if they're unavailable, request that they write a short update for the rest of you to discuss.

We've found the most productive use of these meetings is to:

- BRING UP EVERYTHING THAT'S WORKING WELL, i.e., your child's successes and the approaches that led to them. Provide specific examples of when the school staff shone and went above and beyond. (In addition, you can really help anyone you're grateful to by writing letters about their good works to the head of your district. In the sea of complaints, praise really stands out!) Nothing makes people more excited to keep trying than to know that what they're doing is working well and being appreciated. Have any annual goals or short-term objectives been met and do they therefore require updating? You want progress to continue, and it's good news if goals are moving targets.

- TACKLE ANY CONCERNS. Does anything need to be modified or even scratched completely? Do any goals need to be broken down into easier branch steps to assure achievement?

- DISCUSS WHAT YOU'D LIKE TO SEE HAPPEN GOING FORWARD: Remind everyone of the IEP goals, and if you have suggestions for targeting them more effectively, share those.

- KEEP YOUR CHILD'S SPECIALISTS WORKING AS A TEAM. No one of us is better than another, but we each have different levels of experience, education, and professional training. As long as each team member is putting in the effort and your child is improving, try to keep those services in place. If you notice a team member isn't putting in the effort, get some concrete data.

It's less helpful to say "Ms. Kelly isn't helping my child" than it is to say "I noticed that my child was walking the perimeter of the playground the whole recess period. What social program can we start to encourage his engagement and social conversation?"

- CREATE A WARM ENVIRONMENT. If you have the prep time, it's nice to bring something to the IEP to break the ice and create a welcoming environment. This can be a special drawing your child created, a photo or short video of your child succeeding at a task, a note you or your child wrote about something meaningful, even cookies, muffins, or some other type of treat. Any of these things will mean a lot to school staff and create a warmer, more unified atmosphere for the meeting.

Remember that team meetings should *not* be a bunch of specialists coming together to tell you what your child needs. It should be an opportunity for you to convey your child's wishes, hopes, and needs, so the professionals can work with you and your child to develop the goals and program to achieve those things.

If you're in the middle of the school year and didn't include these types of coordination or update meetings in your IEP, you can request instead that each person working with your child regularly provide you with a short update on how your child is performing on the IEP goals—what's working and what changes would help them learn faster. If the update says "doing well" or "had some interfering behaviors" with no detail, ask for concrete data. Updates need to be objective, not subjective, and trends need to be evaluated. If a child is "doing well," what does that mean? How much progress is being made toward the IEP goals? And any behavior issue needs to be monitored regularly and objectively to assess whether the behavior plan is working.

Regular reports can make a difference in the quality and quantity of support your child is receiving.

Specifics

You want to know in updates (whether they're in person, at team meetings, or written in reports) how your child is doing compared with their baseline, and also compared with their peers.

For example, if your child's baseline showed *no* appropriate comments with peers during recess, and a current probe now shows that your child comments three times during that same period, but peers are commenting twenty to thirty times, then even though you've seen an increase, you'll still want to continue with that goal. The public schools are required (by the Individuals with Disabilities Education Act) to collect regular progress data on your child, so you aren't asking them to do anything they aren't already obligated to do. Furthermore, students perform better in classes where teachers have regular data collection systems, proving the value of accurate and frequent data collection in any classroom.

Make sure the data is collected in natural settings. Some children perform perfectly well on social skills in the SLP's office but have no friends to talk and play with at or after school. This type of performance deficit needs to be measured and addressed, but you won't see it if measurements aren't taken out in the playground or at lunch.

If no one is collecting regular data, ask for more frequent data collection in these settings. You can request video recordings of your child in the classroom and around peers, but be aware that, for privacy reasons, the school may need to inform and get permission from the parents of the other students, as well as from any teachers or staff. If recording *is* possible, make sure the videos are long enough to get a good sample of your child's ongoing behavior and that they include both the times when things are going smoothly and also when they're not, so you can compare and contrast for the best sense of what's going on.

Also, ask that data be collected with and without prompting. If your child responds well with prompting, but reverts back to the baseline levels without prompting, you'll need to discuss a prompt-fading plan. See below for more on this.

MAKE SURE PROMPTS ARE BEING FADED APPROPRIATELY

For each program developed, make sure there's enough prompting initially so your child has the support to use the newly learned behavior frequently. Then you want to see a careful prompt-fading program put in place, so that your child uses the behavior spontaneously and independently.

For example, Sara was learning first words, and the support provider was teaching her to ask her peers for desired items, knowing that would lead to a nice reward for her if she effectively communicated. The provider started out by prompting the entire word, then, once Sara could easily echo it, the provider began simply prompting the first sound of the word. After a few days, the provider was able to just point to the object. Eventually, the provider faded farther away, until no prompting was necessary: Sara was using her words spontaneously and independently.

Fading procedures need to be in place for every program. This should be discussed either when starting a new goal or as soon as your child is successful with the prompts. If your child's responses decline when the prompt is faded, it means that the fading was too fast, and a return to smaller, prompted steps is needed.

Noah's school staff decided it was time to begin fading his program, as he was completing his work without assistance. Unfortunately, they didn't properly train his two aides on how to fade, so they just stopped the support all at once. As a result, he reverted to old off-task behaviors that had previously disappeared, and the aides had to return to full prompting—but this time we provided them with instructions for how to fade slowly and gradually, making adjustments based on Noah's behavior.

Too often an aide will abruptly stop all prompting, without a systematic fading program, because the child has been responding well, but it soon becomes clear that the skill hasn't yet been entirely mastered and the child requires a slower, more thoughtful transition.

If success vanishes when prompts are appropriately and gradually faded, it might mean that the "prompts" were taking the place of independent growth. A teenager, who communicated verbally but mostly for the purposes of getting his needs met, had started to use a communication board, which required a one-on-one aide to support his arm as he typed. He was writing some sophisticated things, but only with the support. On his own, he wasn't communicating through the board. We suggested the aide try looking away from the keyboard, while still bolstering his arm, in case she was unintentionally guiding him. Once the aide couldn't see the keyboard, the student was no longer able to type, suggesting that the aide's arm support probably tipped over into arm *steering*. Rather than learning to communicate, the student was learning to passively surrender communication efforts to someone else. Clearly, that wasn't progress, and it would have made more sense to build on his burgeoning verbal skills.

Over-prompting like this can interfere with learning and cause a child to stop trying. You can help prevent this by checking your child's progress after prompting has been faded: if the behavior falls back to baseline levels, something in the program may need to change.

CELEBRATE TRIUMPHS

Being positive makes people feel appreciated and happy. It also makes everyone feel optimistic and eager to work for even more success. Compliment the people you're working with on any successes. The point of having goals is to achieve them, so celebrate when that happens! Bring and share photographs or short video clips of your child engaging in exceptional things. And it can't hurt to continue that positive feedback even when there isn't a meeting—have your child write or bring a note to a teacher, aide, or specialist, thanking them for their support and/or acknowledging something exceptional they've done.

What Happens If Success Is Elusive?

Again, the IEP is a legally binding document. If there's any IEP violation—meaning that the IEP isn't followed as stated—your child may be eligible for compensatory education. This is a process that requires making an official complaint, but if you've documented the lack of services and can prove your case, your school may be required to double up on services, provide services during vacation periods, or reimburse/pay for private services.

One school's SLP quit abruptly, and it took them months to find a new one, so the school provided additional sessions during the summer to make up the lost time for students whose IEPs included language support.

Of course, you don't want your child to miss out on needed services, so don't wait around if they're not getting services that were mandated in their IEP. Inform the school right away, and, if nothing changes, ask for additional services to help your child make the progress they deserve.

RECORD AND DOCUMENT

Document any lapses you see. For instance, if you stop by the school at lunch, and your child is alone, even though a peer program is supposed to be in place during that time, document this and notify the special education staff in writing. This is especially important if lapses occur repeatedly, as happened to one parent we knew, who volunteered in her child's kindergarten classroom, and reported that his aide was asleep—yes, *asleep*—on several different occasions.

If a teacher or specialist isn't controlling the classroom, and it's total chaos, document that. It isn't easy to change your child's teachers, but clear documentation will go a long way toward helping you get what you need. A coordinated team can make a big difference, but if there's a weak link, your child may not be getting the program they deserve.

FIXING PROBLEMS

Observation is vital, but your first indication that something isn't working right at school may come from your child. If they suddenly start showing anxiety about going to school or want to avoid going altogether, you need to investigate, figure out what's going on, and work with your IEP team to solve it. Implementing motivational teaching strategies, such as choice and natural rewards, often results in a child running *into* the classroom rather than away.

If your child is refusing to go to school because academics are difficult, the teachers may be willing to provide some fun activities upon arrival or add more motivational activities into the curriculum to make being there more appealing. They might also want to break challenging assignments into smaller, more achievable parts.

One student wanted friends badly, but no social support program was provided, and so he spent most of his day alone and hated going to school. Once a peer support program was put in place, he couldn't wait to arrive at school.

If your child is experiencing some teasing, it can be helpful to secure a group of volunteer peers to walk them to class and eat lunch with them. If your child feels isolated, see what activities your school provides at lunch and after school, which your child might be willing—or even eager—to join.

There are lots of ways to create success, but programs and services need to be implemented frequently and consistently to achieve it.

Not every program is effective for every child, so ask to see the data regularly, especially when implementing a new approach. Always give something new time to work: it may take a while to show positive results, and you may see some short-lived increases in undesired behaviors in the meantime. But after a few days, if the undesired behavior isn't decreasing and the desired behaviors aren't increasing, call a meeting and discuss a change in the plan.

MOVE SWIFTLY WHEN BEHAVIORS ARE INTERFERING WITH PROGRESS

If your child is exhibiting meltdowns, aggression, or destructive behaviors, it's important to figure out a plan immediately. Don't let your child's education get shortchanged because of behaviors. Aggression and meltdowns can limit the future of a child, so have your team implement a multi-component program as soon as possible. In most cases, a specialized team of individuals who can evaluate and develop a comprehensive plan is required if these behaviors are evident.

As we discuss in detail in chapter 4 ("Tackling Behaviors That Can Dim Your Child's Bright Light"), research shows that these behaviors continue because in some place, at some times, or with some people, they work. Your child is getting what they want, at least some of the time, using this behavior.

For example, at a meeting for thirteen-year-old Victor, the school suggested that he didn't belong in an inclusion class because of his interrupting behaviors. This surprised us because Victor was generally well behaved. Upon closer observation, it became clear that another student (without autism) was provoking Victor whenever the teacher wasn't looking. He quietly taunted him until Victor couldn't stand it anymore and responded by standing up, screaming, then rolling on the floor, which disrupted the entire class. Victor's behaviors served a function: they got the bully to leave him alone because now the teacher was paying attention. Unfortunately, they also got him removed from his class repeatedly. The bully was also being rewarded for *his* behavior—watching Victor disrupt the class was more exciting than the class itself. It continued for quite a while until a specialist observing the class spotted the bully's taunting. Once the teacher moved the antagonist's desk to the front, where she could keep an eye on him, Victor was able to successfully complete his work each day.

Another student honestly and dutifully admitted to his mother that he yelled "Stop!" at his one-on-one aide to get out of a task, and it was working. There's research showing that service providers tend to decrease the difficulty of the task when a child engages in meltdowns or other interfering behaviors, and clearly this aide was quick to give in.

Obviously, we don't want to reward shows of anger. We want every child to learn. Our preference is to make the assignment more fun and engaging so the student enjoys doing the work, but at the very least, make sure challenging tasks are interspersed with easier ones and that the child knows exactly how much work is required. That way, it's not one long frustration after another, and there's a lot of success to keep the student on task and focused. Your child deserves to have a good education, not just easy tasks that will keep behaviors low. (There's an extended discussion of this in chapter 4, "Tackling Behaviors That Can Dim Your Child's Bright Light.")

If behaviors persist, often the school can bring in a specialist, or an aide or teacher with more training, who can develop a program to reduce these behaviors. Sometimes schools ignore problems until they're out of control, but regular communication with the school staff helps identify the small behaviors that can be addressed with a systematic program before they become serious.

We all have to learn to control our emotions even when we're upset. Learning replacement behaviors, self-management, priming, and positive behavior support systems—all of which are described in chapter 4—will help reduce interfering behaviors and lead your child toward engagement and success.

Your Teacher, Your Child, and You

If you're a parent of a child with ASD, you may feel like a lot of what's happening at school is out of your control, since we often can't choose the teachers our children get and we certainly can't dictate how they run their classrooms.

The good news is that there are ways you *can* improve your child's experience at school. You can work with everyone there to get the kind of teaching that will benefit all students, not just your own. There are certain things that we know produce faster learning, and we always recommend that teachers try out these techniques in their classrooms. If you're a teacher reading this section of the chapter, we hope you recognize the value of these methods. If you're a parent, it will give you a head start toward knowing what kinds of teaching you want to see in your child's classroom and some evidence-based information to pass along whenever possible.

If your child is in a fully included program, your teacher may not have extensive training or experience in special education, but enthusiasm and willingness to learn can make up for that. One of our fully included children had a teacher fresh out of grad school, who had no experience with children with developmental differences, but who was keen to learn how to help the child in her classroom. She sent activities home every night for the next day, spent time with him in the classroom, supported his learning, adjusted the curriculum where necessary (including making activities more challenging for him in the areas in which he excelled), supported his socialization, and successfully targeted IEP goals.

TEACHER REQUESTS

How effectively the IEP is implemented depends a lot on which teacher your child gets. Some teachers want to make sure every goal is pursued. Others don't bother to follow the IEP.

I'm never quite sure why parents of special needs students aren't encouraged to request a teacher who would be a good match with their child and family. With the amount of synchronization required to develop and implement a comprehensive program, it's critical that everyone be comfortable coordinating with one another. Every so often we attend an IEP where the parent is asked if they have a preferred teacher, but more likely the school will say "All our teachers are great," probably because they don't want to suggest that one teacher may be better than another. I strongly encourage you to do what you can to get the best teacher for your child. Here are some tips for pursuing that goal without ruffling any feathers.

Before the new school year starts, ask the special education director and school principal for a teacher who understands that your child needs close and regular contact (parents of older students can be helpful with suggestions). This kind of attentiveness may be difficult for some teachers to manage, for a variety of reasons, so it's important to be up-front about the extra effort that will be necessary to bring out the best in your child. There are teachers whom you never hear from unless there's a scheduled parent-teacher conference or report card, and others who are so in touch with the family on a daily basis that they become lifelong friends. You want the latter. We've seen teachers who post the next day's assignment every night so that the parents can preview it, and others who complain about any extra effort asked of them. Enthusiasm, willingness, and effort make a big difference, so try to establish whether the teacher has these qualities beforehand.

It's best to be specific, too. If priming and team meetings are a part of your child's IEP, make sure the teacher knows this well in advance, so they can decide if they can follow through with those. Coordination and communication are critical to bring out your child's potential. Be specific about why a teacher would be a good or not-good match. If there are objective reasons, like the style of discipline, let that be known.

One family we worked with wasn't given the teacher they had requested; Sunny was placed instead in the classroom of a teacher known for loudly and firmly instructing the students to manage their behavior. This was a disaster: Sunny was overwhelmed by loud noises, and the teacher's raised voice made it impossible for her to focus.

If your school doesn't seem to be interested in your attempts to request a specific teacher, at least try to speak up if you know that a teacher *wouldn't* be a good match. Again, be specific. Tell the school why your child's learning style or your family values aren't compatible with any given teacher—when there's a well-reasoned argument, they're more likely to see the wisdom of a different placement. We all want to drop off our kids at school and feel happy about that. If you don't have a good teacher, you'll worry that you're shortchanging your child each and every day.

GOOD TEACHER/BAD TEACHER

We've all seen movies about "bad" teachers—ones who can't manage the kids and are just counting down the days until summer. We've also seen the "good teacher" movies. Those teachers inspire and transform the children with a combination of skill, tough love, and tenacity. They believe in their students and would do almost anything to help them reach their potential.

In films, it's easy to spot a good or bad teacher, but in real life? Not always so easy.

The main measurement we have of a good teacher is whether a

child is learning, based on tests, report cards, and teacher conferences. We evaluate a child's happiness with the teacher primarily on that child's reporting.

But, to be honest, it isn't easy to measure teacher competence in any objective way. Parents and students like different teachers for different reasons; coworkers click with one teacher or another because of personality; principals and staff have preferences that may not be based on teaching skill. Additionally, teachers—although they aren't supposed to—play favorites. They're human. So a student who happens to fit a teacher's desired mold may prosper in that classroom, while a student who doesn't may find that they're not getting the attention or support they need.

There's new research coming out on best teaching practices every day. Busy teachers often don't have time to read the latest literature, but the ones who find a way to do so will have more evidenced-based strategies to draw from. The research clearly shows that not every child has the same response to any given approach, so if a specific strategy isn't leading to progress, a teacher's skill set needs to be broad enough for them to pivot to a new strategy, or a combination of strategies. It's important to be respectful of your teacher's busy schedule, so if you're a parent and have time to keep up on the literature, share any helpful knowledge with them (ideally, in a nonconfrontational, noncritical way—we're talking *constructive* support here).

The Best Classroom Techniques

We've observed a lot of classrooms and we've seen what works well with students and what doesn't. And we're not just talking about children with differences—*all* kids want and deserve a teacher who keeps things fun and interesting.

Here's what we're looking for when we talk about successful teaching:

A POSITIVE APPROACH

Some teachers control their classroom with specific threats ("Derek, if you don't sit down, I'll send you to the principal's office"), demanding language ("Sandy, you need to get to work!"), and/or a scary raised voice ("I want it quiet. NOW"). Students who are controlled through punishment or fear often *will* behave, but at a loss to their self-esteem and comfort.

We want children to behave because it feels rewarding to them, not because they're afraid of being punished. We want good role models for our children: we don't want them to think that anger and threats are appropriate in the classroom.

Look for teachers who use positive strategies frequently and punishment infrequently. Positive strategies rely on seeking out and rewarding helpful behaviors, such as, "I like the way Remy is sitting!" "Thank you for getting right to work, Gina!" "Jason, Mindy, and Ashley are standing in line so nicely . . . oh, so are Johnny, Brent, and Cindy!" Most students will respond swiftly to positive recognition.

If a teacher asks a student to engage in a new behavior, but then doesn't follow through by checking and redirecting if the child doesn't respond, the child will quickly learn that sitting back and ignoring the teacher makes life a whole lot easier. The teacher needs to stay on top of every situation, repeating instructions when necessary and gently leading the child to respond. Setting this course in the beginning and sticking to it will reduce behavior issues and any need for discipline because the child has failed to respond at a later, possibly more crucial moment.

Having a positive, thoughtful approach affects academic success as well as behavior. We recently helped out in a classroom where the lesson was about how animals camouflage themselves. Following the discussion, the students were asked to color a picture of a camouflaged animal. One little girl drew a pink bunny camouflaged amid beautiful pink foliage. The teacher, to our horror, criticized the student's work with a brusque "Rabbits aren't pink." But the student had thoroughly grasped the concept of camouflage and deserved to be commended, not chastised. Not having their good work recognized may well mean that a student doesn't even bother to try to fulfill the next assignment—what's the point?

Observing another classroom, we noted that within the first ten minutes after our arrival, the teacher had already said at least eight negative things. One boy expressed concern about a jacket he'd found that his friend in another class might be looking for. Rather than complimenting him on his empathy, the teacher snapped, "We aren't going to worry about a jacket right now." She also told the entire class, "Do you think I want you to come up and ask me questions that you should know the answer to?" Wow. Talk about discouraging children from wanting to understand everything they can! She probably didn't even realize she was creating an environment where students felt discouraged and were losing interest in engaging. Frustratingly, she had student teachers who were learning how to run a class from her, so her negativity was going to extend past her own classroom into future ones.

Everyone wants to be rewarded, praised for their strengths, and encouraged. Finding a teacher who's positive, dedicated, and supportive is important for your child's success and self-worth.

MOTIVATIONAL LEARNING

Similarly, motivational procedures—building on a child's strengths and interests—will foster learning and nurture self-confidence. You want your child's teacher to understand this and to naturally incorporate the concepts your child (and other students, too) already gravitate toward. For all students, practical hands-on activities are the most fun and most memorable learning experiences.

Some ways we've seen teachers do this include:

- Having students write a personal letter to a grandparent, aunt, family friend, or other favorite person to improve penmanship, instead of copying form letters. They can learn other important things, such as where the address, stamp, and return address go on an envelope (and if the address isn't legible, they'll learn the letter will be returned—natural consequences!). They may even get a letter back (a natural reward!).

- When working on reading, letting the child choose their own book, ideally with a subject they want to know more about, so reading becomes a naturally rewarding activity.

- Adding up prices from a catalogue (where you get to choose the items you want) for a math lesson. A child who might run away from a math worksheet is likely to come running to the desk if it's holding a catalog of favorite items instead.

- Doubling a recipe of a favorite treat to learn fractions or using a menu from a favorite restaurant to learn how to calculate tips and/or taxes. These activities are fun and meaningful.

- Teaching percentages with M&Ms: the students can divvy up the colors and figure out the percentage of each one in a bowl or bag. Mean, median, mode, and graphing can also be taught with a small bag of M&Ms. There's no better way to capture attention than with a desired treat.

- Providing bus and train schedules, which can offer a lot of different learning opportunities, as can a simple clock (how much longer until recess?). These assignments are practical, too.

The sky's the limit: it's about being creative and looking for real-life opportunities rather than printing up a bunch of worksheets.

CHOICE

Similarly, if students can exercise some choice over their activities, they'll be more engaged and will work harder. (This is true for all of us, by the way: having some control makes us more invested in any task.) A teacher should provide choice whenever possible, but—just to be clear—we're not talking about the choice of whether or not to participate. We're talking about specific, limited choices, ones that get the students excited about the activity.

Does it really matter *what* the students are reading, writing, or spelling so long as they're learning to read and write and spell? If students are gravitating toward reading certain books on their own, or are fascinated by certain subjects, then those texts can be used for reading, instead of something someone else decided would be "educational."

And it also makes sense to use child-chosen topics for writing, even if it's short sentences, such as "I want to play on the computer," which can be rewarded with access right after. These types of natural rewards make the task meaningful.

A teacher who offers reasonable choices, whenever possible, is likely to have students who feel respected and engaged.

GOOD PACING

Teachers who don't keep things moving and who talk too much (or too little) can be tough for students to stay attentive to. During class time, teachers should keep up a brisk pace that sustains the students' interest. Sometimes we go into classrooms and the pace is so slow that even we observers struggle to stay awake!

Look for teachers who are ready to go when class starts and keep things moving until the end of the period: a few minutes wasted before each class can really add up.

One teacher we knew was always the last to collect her students after the bell rang, and then had to spend several minutes getting them to settle down. By the time she started the lesson, five to ten minutes had passed. Over the course of the school year, hundreds of minutes of classroom time had been wasted and lost forever.

In contrast, another teacher at the same school used every minute she could for teaching. For example, when walking to a special class, she played fun games with her students, calling out orders such as "Put your ulna on your cranium!," "Put your distal phalange on your zygomatic bone!," or "Walk on your calcaneus!" It was fun for the kids, and they all picked up a lot of knowledge about human anatomy, without even realizing it.

EMPLOYING PARTIAL PARTICIPATION WHEN HELPFUL

Every child should be doing assignments at their own level; noting and taking into account a child's individual needs and abilities will bring out their best. If the regular education curriculum is too difficult for a student, the teacher should know how to modify it.

This concept is similar to how chores are distributed in homes with children of different ages. For example, while loading the dishwasher, the littlest family member wouldn't be the one to put in the china, glasses, or knives. The littlest one puts the spoons in. The important thing is that the littlest one *is* participating and learning how to load the dishwasher—just at their own level.

Children with autism can and should be exposed to the same curriculum as their peers in regular education, but at the maximum level they can succeed at. For example, if students in the classroom are learning how to add double digits, but the student with ASD is still working on single digits, the same math problem can be adjusted:

Example:

$$41$$
$$+29$$

adjusted for single digits

```
  1
+9
```

Teachers should know how to adjust the curriculum for partial participation for all academic subjects: math, reading, history, geography, and so on. There are books, articles, booklets, and websites that describe partial participation, and degreed teachers should have learned this information. It's critical to understand that partial participation does *not* mean that students will have their own separate curriculum. Partial participation means that students will learn, to the best of their capabilities, what's expected at that grade level. Students with ASD often have areas where they excel and other areas where they struggle: partial participation in the weaker areas allows them to stay in an environment where they can exhibit their strengths and keep moving forward.

We often visit classrooms that have a child with ASD included for the full day, but the child is seated away from the other children and is being given a completely different curriculum. This isn't "inclusion": this is a separate class that happens to be set inside another classroom. We want all our students to be involved, engaged, active, and successful—and partial participation is a great tool to get them there.

ORGANIZATION

An organized teacher has an edge over a disorganized one. It's not the only trait that matters, but it is an important one. Most teachers prepare lesson plans ahead of time, so they're ready to start as soon as class begins. It also means they can share materials and subject matter ahead of time, which can make a huge difference to students who benefit from priming.

Teachers also need to be able to organize a safe and productive classroom environment, with materials and furniture optimally arranged for both efficiency and comfort. A tidy and well-arranged classroom means teachers can easily monitor and track their students, collecting data when necessary for IEP goals, as we discussed earlier.

Teachers should be aware of specific student needs and have a planned response: if your child has a tendency to slip away from the classroom when he's bored, the teacher may want to assign them a seat near her so she can keep tabs on them. And if peer support is on the IEP, the teacher should think about placing a student with ASD near a student known to be helpful and supportive.

All students are more comfortable knowing what's expected of them, and an organized teacher is more likely to make that clear.

ENGAGEMENT

Some classroom teachers will use one-on-one aides as a go-between, rather than engage directly with the students who have them. Maybe they believe the other students need their attention more, since there's already an adult in place for the students with special needs; maybe they simply want to take the easy route. Either way, it's not an ideal situation: we want all students to learn to take instruction directly from the teacher, to listen with the group, and to engage in classroom dialogues. A teacher should interact positively and directly with each and every student in their classroom.

If you haven't received a daily schedule, ask for one—which every teacher has—but also ask which instructor will be responsible for the teaching during each activity. This way, you'll know which teacher you should communicate with if an issue arises. And, just like the homeroom or lead teacher, any specialty teacher should be engaging directly with your child, not just addressing the aide.

OPEN CLASSROOM, OPEN MIND

We worked with one family whose kindergarten teacher wouldn't let any parent volunteer: he had a strange and unusual policy that excluded parents from the classroom. He also checked all the boxes on a bad teacher: no control in the classroom, too much down time, terrible home-school coordination. We could see why he didn't want anyone in the classroom: parents weren't likely to approve of what was going on there.

In our experience, teachers who welcome observations and collaboration and invite parents into their classroom are likely to have well-coordinated and effective programs. Transparency is a sign that things are working well—and an invitation to work together to make things even better. See if you can help in the classroom—even just once a week will be helpful—or at least visit to observe. And no matter what, make sure there's coordination between school and home and that the IEP goals are being implemented.

A FEW MORE WAYS TO MAKE CLASSROOM TIME
BETTER FOR EVERYONE

- Varying activities frequently will improve student engagement. Studies show that children respond better if the academics are varied, and they don't have to repeat the same exact task over and over again. Variety keeps things interesting. That doesn't mean teachers have to bop around among subjects (although short, interspersed learning periods are fine), just that they should vary activities within each subject.

- Physical activity, like stretch exercises or a run around the campus, will break up a lesson and help students focus.

- Alternating challenging tasks with ones that the students have already mastered will give children a sense of accomplishment and success, so they'll stay engaged and feel empowered to tackle new challenges.

- Pairing autistic students with non-autistic classmates as they walk together from one activity to another will give them a chance to interact, socialize, and talk. For verbal children, the teacher can suggest each duo ask each other specific questions, like how many siblings they have, what their favorite dessert is, what TV shows they like, etc.

- Using cooperative arrangements during activities will increase social engagement. For instance, if a class is stringing beads to make necklaces, instead of giving everyone a mixed bowl of colored beads, a teacher can separate out the different colors, so the children need to ask one another to pass the beads they want. Both questions ("Can you please pass the red beads?") and responses ("Sure, here they are") can be prompted. If children are playing with blocks, they can be paired so that one holds the blocks while the other asks for them. All these little strategies will help your child blossom into feeling socially confident and connected.

Aides

If your child has a paraprofessional/aide/support person, really get to know them, since they're spending a lot of time with your child. Include them in all team meetings, and if they can't attend, give them a recap afterward.

Too often, people hired as aides don't have the extensive expertise or focus that we might wish for. For instance, Kamal came home one day with no eyelashes on either eye. When his mother asked him what happened, he said that he had cut them off with scissors during math. His mother was understandably concerned that he had been able to do something so risky without his full-time one-on-one aide even noticing! It's also fairly common for aides to stand back or chat with other adults during recess rather than assist with inclusion in games and activities, which would be far more beneficial for their students.

While it's hard to screen for who'll be an effective support person, almost everyone will need some training. Special education staff can be helpful with training aides, and most schools will allow outside providers to visit on occasion to coordinate goals.

Everyone has "off days," but when aides lack energy and aren't engaged, a change may be needed. If you have concerns, talk to the aide first. Often the aides are very open to suggestions and willing to make adjustments. If that doesn't work, or if the district discourages you from talking directly to the aide, discuss the need for individualized training with the aide's supervisor. Resources are often available for specialized training. The aide may also be able to sit in on some sessions with more specialized providers, like the SLP or program specialist.

It's important to make sure that aides are actively providing services since they're with your child most of the day. If you have concerns that the aide has become lax, make sure data is being collected both when your child is with the aide and when they're not, so the two sets can be compared. You can also request that an outside specialist or consultant go to the school to observe. If it's documented that the aide isn't effective, you can request a change.

While most aides are enthusiastic and eager to get more training, there are some who just aren't cut out for the job or who don't work well with a particular child's individual and unique needs. Your child will benefit greatly if the aide is well trained and committed to implementing goals throughout the day.

Specialists

If you find that a school specialist isn't a good match with your child, you can opt out of their services, or use them for consulting instead of direct services. One well-meaning specialist admitted to a student's parents that she really didn't know how to control their child, who acted up throughout the session. This was one specialty class the parents graciously opted out of.

But when things are going well, make sure you acknowledge that, too—many school staff members feel undervalued and underappreciated. We all have a tendency to complain when there's a problem and to assume that smooth sailing is the "norm," but often people are working very hard for that smooth sailing. Let the people who are working well with your child know that you see and appreciate what they do all year long. No one minds an unexpected compliment or thank you!

Why Every Detail Matters

We want our kids engaged, motivated, involved, and connected. The right people with the right guidance and training will make that happen.

Here are some examples of missed opportunities we've seen. These bright kids deserved better.

- Kevin's aide yelled at him to "Get back on the playground!" when he tried to slip out into the parking lot to memorize license plates, something he loved and was interested in. Instead of scolding him, we identified Kevin's interest, and created a license plate game for him and the other children to play together, which led to more socializing and a chance to display Kevin's talents.

- Jamie's aide in kindergarten only interceded when there was a conflict. We worked collaboratively with the school to train his aide to prompt communication by teaching Jamie to comment, ask questions, share toys, and compliment his peers throughout his play. This eliminated the conflicts, and increased his social communication during unstructured activities.

- Fifth-grader Devon's teacher had her take a walk whenever Devon rebelled at doing her schoolwork, rather than finding the time to figure out how to motivate and interest her. Devon had learned to ask for a "motor break" every time the teacher started an activity she didn't like and was spending most of her academic time walking the perimeter of the playground with the classroom aide. We encouraged the teacher to create some motivational academic activities by including Devon's interests, so Devon could stay engaged and display her innate brilliance.

We've seen well-trained teachers and aides encourage and engage students, both academically and socially, allowing them to blossom. Every moment in your child's education counts, and so we've provided suggestions on how to understand what to ask for, how to ask for it, and how to make sure your child's strengths are nurtured and developed both at school and at home.

SUMMARY

We discussed a lot in this chapter, but the most important thing to remember is that your child deserves to have a coordinated program with good teaching. If your child isn't learning something, first ask if the teaching strategies can be changed. Often a child isn't learning because the best teaching techniques aren't being implemented, or aren't being implemented properly. Next, make sure that there's regular data collection of your child's behavior and progress. If a child isn't learning quickly (or at all) this tracking will tell us we need to change something, whether it's synchronizing the program, breaking it into smaller pieces, or adjusting the teaching strategies. Most importantly, make sure your child is having fun learning. If a teacher isn't making progress with your child, too often it's because strengths and interests haven't been tapped, and your child simply isn't motivated.

This means you have to know your stuff—at least a little bit. The more you know about options for your child, the more readily you can suggest evidence-based game changers, like motivational programs, peer mediation, social communication, priming, and curriculum modifications. You don't have to be an expert, but, surprisingly, many "professionals" haven't learned to implement some helpful strategies.

Also, remember that the IEP is a critical (and legal) document. If it isn't in the IEP, it may not happen, so make sure the things that are most important to your child and your family are included. Your child's strengths, interests, and desires need to be the focus of every learning activity to bring out their full potential.

Finally, maintain open and frequent communication with the school. Most professionals and teachers want to do what's best for your child, and that's more likely to happen if every success and accomplishment is shared and you work through challenges as a team.

Remember, no one knows what the future of your child will be. But it's only when everyone aims high that the best outcomes can be realized.

CHAPTER 6

In-Home Programs

YOUR HOUSE, YOUR RULES, YOUR GOALS

Many children with autism are eligible to receive programs that are provided in their own home through insurance or state-funded programs. These in-home programs, when run by high-quality and well-trained staff, can simplify life by reducing your travel time to and from various services and providing support in your child's natural setting—and that's important. Sometimes children on the autism spectrum learn to respond only in a particular setting or with specific items, but don't generalize that newly learned response to different situations. Having programs in the child's home can mitigate these generalization issues. In-home programs take place in the child's natural home setting, and siblings and neighborhood peers can be recruited to help with teaching turn-taking, socialization, and communication. Additionally, the provider can work on important daily living skills, including dressing, cleaning up, and doing the laundry. So many of our kids are capable of performing well in their everyday settings, and we want to build on that to make sure they shine where they're most comfortable. With practice, they'll be able to broaden their comfort zone and become more confident and capable everywhere they go. Many parents say in-home services are a lifesaver, so finding the right program match is important.

Making Sure Your Home Program Is Top-Notch

Children with autism are usually eligible for services in their homes, but there can be some challenges in setting them up. We'll explore these potential pitfalls quickly, so we can move on to discussing how to avoid them and develop a successful in-home program.

Just as in schools—where a minimally trained aide may be the adult the children work with the most—many of the in-home day-to-day providers don't have a strong education or extensive experience in special education. They may well have some amazing skills, but, with limited formal education, they need to rely on a supervisor to help them develop goals, a step-by-step teaching program, and a system for monitoring the effectiveness of that program. Fortunately, they *do* have supervisors, and knowing they can use some guidance will spur you on to provide suggestions.

As with school staff, there's a lot of turnover: it often feels like just when a provider is working well with your child, they find another job or get hired full-time by another family. Because there's so much turnover, and training is time-consuming and costly, agencies often opt for "on-the-job training," which means they can bill for the hours the untrained provider is working with your child.

You definitely want your provider's time to be meaningful, because it can be a bit of a strain when someone new comes into your home on a daily basis. You may feel the pressure of tidying up, wearing something presentable, greeting them at the door, making sure there are drinks and snacks available, and just knowing that your family and your house are on display.

Then there's the question of how effective the match is. There are some providers whom everyone loves, some who fit with certain families and not others, and, disappointingly, some who just aren't cut out for working with autistic children.

We've seen every one of these situations firsthand. For instance, we had a graduate student whom families either loved or hated. Some parents requested her specifically and others asked to switch to someone else. She liked to roughhouse with the kids, which worked great for some families and was off-putting to others. We learned to only place her with kids who loved physical interaction (and families who approved of it).

Finally, too many providers are trained in structured drill-type procedures, as these are often easier to train quickly than the more effective naturalistic ones. This leads them to follow a specific structured protocol so closely that they don't seem to take into account the individual child's needs, wants, preferences, and choices.

Finding a good match is important, since this person will be with your child on a regular basis for a lot of hours, so don't settle for something that's not working.

Of course, that can be easier said than done—I've had parents tell me that they have concerns about their provider, but if they change agencies, they'll be put on a wait list and their child may go without assistance for a possibly lengthy time period. If you do have someone who isn't a good fit, you may want to see if the company has another provider you could try out before you ask to switch agencies.

There are quite a few things you can do—both before you get matched with a provider and after—to obtain the best possible match for your child and avoid the frustrations described above.

INTERVIEW

Starting off with the right agency will make a difference in the success of the program, so check your options thoroughly before committing to one. Usually insurance companies will provide you with a list of providers they work with in your area. Before you settle on one, ask for an interview, and, if possible, bring your child, so you can see how well the candidate engages with them right from the start. Here are some questions that you can ask:

- How often is the day-to-day provider supervised?

- Who will be supervising the program?

- Is supervision in person or remote? (In person is better, because the supervisor can provide feedback on the nuances of the session.)

- What training and experience do the supervisor and in-home provider have? (Most supervisors will have a master's degree and in many states will also be licensed or certified.)

- How many providers will be assigned to your child? For example, if your child is authorized to receive twenty hours a week, are these hours provided by one person or several?

- Is there a policy that allows you to try out providers to see if they're a good match?

- Are providers trained on motivational procedures?

- Is parent education provided? Will providers work to coordinate the program with you so you can work on skills during your daily routine?

- Will the supervisor be able and willing to coordinate with the school?

- If a provider is sick, goes away on vacation, or quits, is a substitute provided?

- Is the provider allowed to take your child outside of the home for work in the local park, stores, or other locations, if warranted?

- Are motivational techniques used during the sessions?

COMMUNICATE YOUR GOALS FROM THE START

Start—immediately, in this very first meeting—listing goals that are important to you, ones that will make your child's and family's life easier. Think long term and don't hesitate to focus on life skills. It's probably more important to you that your child learn to brush their teeth and dress independently than to know how to stack blocks. But an in-home provider might stick to the latter if that's how they've been trained. Learning how to prepare a snack, feed the dog, sort the laundry, etc., are all great goals for your child's eventual independence.

We worked with a college student who had never washed his own laundry and, while living on his own, automatically removed his clothes from the dryer after a single cycle, even if they were still wet. Consequently, his pile of clothes collected mildew and, well . . . he never smelled that great. Once we figured out the problem, we were able to help him learn that if the clothes are still wet, you can run them through a second or third drying cycle. This could—and should—have been something he learned as a child, for both his sake and his family's.

If you need some quiet time to help another child with homework, ask that a designated period of each in-home visit be dedicated to outdoor or quiet activities. If your child needs to learn how to socialize, insist that structured playdates be implemented on a regular basis.

Also, keep in mind that if your child is young and not talking yet, verbal communication must be a primary focus. The more that your child can communicate, the easier their life will be; they deserve to be able to express their needs and have them met. We've seen too many programs that missed precious opportunities to practice, prompt, and teach communication, working instead on areas like joint attention, imitation, or eye contact—all of which usually fall into place naturally once a child learns social communication. Your child is capable of so much, but if they lack the tools to communicate their thoughts and knowledge, they may not be able to achieve everything they want to. (Chapter 3, "Communication: The Bridge That Connects," goes into much greater detail about this.)

If your child does fine at home but demonstrates behaviors out in the world that make it impossible for you to take them on outings, improving this should be a goal for your in-home provider. Step-by-step programs that incorporate motivational components—such as starting with having your child purchase a favorite food item at the grocery store—will help your child learn to enjoy going out. For many families, this is likely to be a priority.

Goals are individual, and some may not be obvious to the providers. We've had families suggest important goals that we might never have thought of.

Here are some examples of what we mean when we talk about personal goals:

- One mom worked at night and was stressed about packing her son's lunch, so our providers taught him how to pack it himself.

- One family's son was so noisy that they couldn't attend church, so their in-home providers worked on a program for "quiet time" at church.

- Another parent loved to cook and wanted their son to be part of that experience, so their in-home providers taught him to measure, pour, and stir. He not only learned about fractions but was positively rewarded when he could taste the batter or eat the delicious treat he had helped make.

- One mother wanted her son to participate in sports, but he didn't enjoy them, so we taught him to cheer on his peers instead, which made them delighted to have him at games.

- A family wanted their son to learn how to play games with the neighborhood kids in the alley where they all congregated after school and noted that he longingly watched them out the window. The in-home provider moved the bulk of their time outside, where she could encourage him to join in and get comfortable socializing.

As you can see, all these families had specific, disparate goals, with one thing in common: improving their child's time with them and others. Let your providers know exactly what would make your family life a happier one and follow through to make sure these goals are part of the program and implemented correctly.

STICK TO FAMILY RULES

Service providers differ wildly in their approaches: some are playful, and others are more serious. Some prefer working indoors, and others outside. Some are tidy, and others are fine with a mess of toys everywhere. It's important to make a list of family rules that are important to *you*, that you'd like them to stick to and reinforce with your child. They don't have to be major rules, just things that matter to you.

Having someone in your home day in and day out is a lifestyle change, and if the household rules and your needs are clear from the beginning, everyone will be happier. For example, if you want the toy room to stay organized, make sure the provider teaches your child to put away each toy before moving to the next. If some areas of the house are "off limits" or need to stay quiet, make sure the people coming to your home understand that.

We worked with one family whose provider rewarded the child for completing his homework by letting him run through the house squealing and screaming. His parents found the noise overwhelming, so the provider made a simple switch to having the child celebrate outside.

In-home services should be a support to you and your child. If something is increasing your stress level, calmly and kindly bring up a suggestion for substituting, adding, or modifying the activities so they fit more smoothly into your preferred household routines.

MAKE IT FUN

If your child cries when the provider comes or tries to avoid the sessions, ask the provider to incorporate your child's favorite toys, activities, and items into the program. Your child deserves to enjoy learning. Responding just to avoid a punishment will never create a motivated and enthusiastic learner. Most providers learn to deal with behaviors without using punishment (which is obviously a requirement), but one who's simply not inspiring still needs to improve. You want to see smiles, laughter, engagement, and happy responding from your child, not crying, avoidance, escape, frowns, and discontent, so change things quickly if you're getting the latter.

TEACHING SKILLS WHERE THEY'RE NEEDED

We've discussed the importance of "natural settings" before, so you know that sometimes you have to move learning out of the classroom. If you have in-home services and there are social goals, make sure that the service provider takes your child to settings (park, beach, playground, etc.) where peers interact, or that the provider invites peers for playdates, where the provider can prompt play engagement and social conversation.

When my nephew had a hard time waiting his turn and socializing with the other children in kindergarten, my daughter spent an extra half hour after school with him each day on the playground, where the children congregated before going home, prompting his social conversation skills while also teaching him how to patiently wait for his turn. That little half hour of daily support made a huge difference.

EDUCATE YOURSELF

You don't have to get a degree in psychology or speech and language to help your child, but you should stay up on the latest scientific, evidence-based research. Your child doesn't have time to waste. They need to be getting support in ways that have been shown scientifically to be effective. We see "new" approaches to autism popping up all the time on social media and in the news; people get excited about them, but once they're researched, they're found to be ineffective. Put your trust in professionals who use tried-and-true, evidence-based, researched approaches. And make sure the programs support your child in a positive way—with playfulness and plenty of praise for trying.

Knowledge will help you guide your providers rather than just blindly trust that they've been correctly trained, which, as we've discussed, isn't always the case. In-home programs should include a weekly parent education session—most insurance companies require this—when the provider can fill you in on what they've been working on and how it's going.

It's important to set aside time every week to observe your provider, if even briefly, while they're working with your child. (See below for more on this.) If you're feeling unsure about a provider, record a session, so you can ask the supervisor or another person you trust to assess if they need more training. Are they providing enough opportunities for learning? Are they using motivational components? Are they rewarding your child frequently? Is their demeanor inviting and pleasing to your child? Are meaningful goals being taught?

Ask to see the data regularly. Insurance companies will ask the provider for data, some on a monthly basis, and what you're seeing should match the data. In other words, if an in-home provider is claiming your child has gained skills, make sure you're seeing those skills in action.

Additionally, supervisors of in-home programs should attend your school meetings as often as possible. If there's an approach that's helping your child in school, but your provider isn't using it, discuss it with the supervisor. You know your child well, and how to bring out their best, so anything the provider doesn't see should be pointed out.

BE THERE. BE INVOLVED.

I'm still shocked when parents report that a provider has asked them not to be present during the sessions. Sometimes there's an excuse— "He performs better if you're not around" or "She gets too excited when you're here"—but sometimes it's just a simple dismissal and an "I'll bring you up to speed later."

If it's true that your child is more responsive when you aren't there, you should be learning what methods the provider is using to engage them so you can also have them in your toolbox—and you'll only learn this by attending the sessions.

There are a lot of reasons the provider might be keeping you out of the sessions. Some might feel insecure about their abilities and don't feel comfortable with parents watching. Others haven't had explicit training for working with parents and aren't sure how they're supposed to interact with you.

In the first situation, you definitely want to observe to make sure everything is going smoothly. If you suspect the second reason, reassure the provider that you're there to support and learn from them, not to criticize.

In all fairness, sometimes too much parent input *can* be challenging, especially if a parent is a micromanager or comes across as critical. You're the expert on your child, of course, but do keep in mind that different approaches can be beneficial, and other people are sometimes competent in ways that might differ from yours.

If you get the sense that you're overwhelming a provider during their sessions with too many questions and critiques, consider scheduling regular meetings that are separate from the working sessions. Then you'll have time and freedom to ask questions, share video of successful moments with your child that the provider may not be aware of, discuss what you feel is and isn't working, and allow your provider to explain their approach and why it may differ from yours.

Just as your child is unique, so is every clinician, and giving them a chance to explain why they're choosing to do something in a certain way can be enormously helpful to you both. Open minds on both sides will help you home in on what works best for your child.

It shouldn't be necessary to attend every entire session (in fact, you should enjoy the break now and then), but you do need to be an integral part of the support all along the way. Your child will fare better if you're informed and can provide input, coordinate the goals, and follow through with any effective strategies. You're with your child after hours, on the weekend, during holidays, and for the rest of their life. Don't let anyone exclude you from participating. Make sure your comments are helpful and supportive. It's teamwork, and you have valuable input, knowledge, and skills to contribute.

INCLUDE YOUR OTHER CHILDREN

I've visited families where siblings begged to join the session but were told they weren't allowed. This has never made sense to me. Children learning social communication should be encouraged to interact with other children, and brothers and sisters can be a great source of assistance with this.

They can also help with specific goals, like language acquisition: since they're always around, if they learn to prompt words and respond quickly to attempts, they'll be able to support progress even when the provider isn't around.

Exclusion fosters resentment, whereas enthusiastic praise and admiration for helping and participating foster a close sibling relationship. The involvement and support of siblings can work across settings (like at school or out at a park) in a way the adults' may not, and they can also accurately model how to socialize with similarly aged children in a way adults can't.

Always remember to praise your children when they're being kind and helpful. Everyone appreciates a compliment, hug, or acknowledgment when they've gone out of their way. And you want them to value and enjoy their time with their sibling and feel like that connection matters.

SUMMARY

First and foremost, your home is your sanctuary, and you and your family deserve to feel comfortable there. Don't hesitate to express what's important to you, to make the house rules clear, and to be explicit about the long-term and short-term goals you have for your child.

If you feel like your child is being drilled or not having fun, ask that motivational procedures be included in the program.

Most in-home providers, particularly supervisors, need to take continuing education courses each year that are specifically for autism, so ask about the newest strategies and the latest research in any area that's relevant to your child—you'll know more about what they're doing and learn more about what *you* can do.

We want goals to be coordinated across all settings, so ask your in-home provider to attend your IEP and make sure there's information flowing between what's happening in your home and at the school. The provider should be a big part of this.

As always, your child's strengths, interests, and desires should be the focus of every learning activity. Fortunately, most in-home program supervisors are required to provide parent education each week, so while you're discussing what's working and what's not, take this opportunity to make any changes and adjustments. A collaborative and open process is essential in bringing out your child's potential.

CHAPTER 7

Community Matters

If there's one fact we want you to take away from this book, it's this one: diversity enriches a community. A society that doesn't recognize this simple truth will fail to thrive.

From the classroom to the boardroom, a variety of experiences and viewpoints brings a healthy perspective and the kinds of challenges to the status quo that lead to innovation and inspiration. Many of us know this instinctively, but research also bears it out.

So why does our society make it so hard to be different?

There's no simple answer to this very complicated question. One explanation is "tribalism," but that's an answer that only makes us wonder why, since human beings are capable of profound thought and understanding, we're still clinging to beliefs that no longer serve us, and that date from prehistoric times, when to wander away from your tiny, family-based community meant danger and probably death.

All we know for sure is that everyone's life would be improved vastly if we could all learn to embrace diversity.

We're on a mission to make the world a more inclusive place, and we hope you'll join us in that, for the sake of our children, our friends, and our community.

Neurodiversity

Diversity can come in a lot of different forms. In this book, we are, of course, particularly concerned with neurodiversity—neurological differences that express themselves in a vast spectrum of behaviors.

A sad truth is that even people who are welcoming toward those with physical differences will often judge and pull away from someone whose behaviors don't fit into their idea of "normal" (whatever that may be). It's not fair and it's not right, but virtually every single person with neurological differences has at some point experienced negative judgment out in public, and that's usually equally true for their companions, family, friends, support staff, whoever.

As a community, we have to push for education, understanding, tolerance, and respect in each and every social interaction. There's no other way to make life better for us all, and to show our support for those with any kind of difference. But change comes slowly and not everyone is open to learning.

That's the frustrating news.

The good news is that we have some ideas about how to improve your life out in the world with your neurodiverse child. And we're hopeful you will internalize the following message and carry it with you wherever you go: you and your child deserve respect and support.

Improving the Quality of Life for All of Us

Having a high quality of life (QoL) is important for everyone, and especially important for families of children with ASD, who work tirelessly to support their wonderful children. But because people are often uncomfortable with behavioral differences, or don't fully understand them, they may either exclude families of children with ASD or be judgmental of them which, sadly, can affect families' QoL.

This creates a vicious cycle (yes, we know, we talk a lot about cycles in this book: that's because we see so many, both for the better and the worse): the more a family can participate in social activities, the better for their children's socialization skills. But the kids who are most in need of improving their social skills are the ones whose families are made to feel unwelcome in social situations. The parents understandably withdraw; the child doesn't get the kind of socialization opportunities they most need; the child's social skills don't improve; any attempt to socialize continues to be challenging; the parents withdraw even more.

We don't blame parents for wanting to avoid exposing themselves or their child to unpleasant, even punishing scenarios. Many parents have told us of strangers approaching them in public with advice or harsh words when they're doing their best to deal with a difficult situation, adding humiliation to an already tough time. You don't have to have a child with differences to know that whenever a child misbehaves in public, the world is eager to condemn the accompanying adult for their "bad parenting." We find this astounding, given that many parenting experts encourage parents not to give in to tantrums, so they're not inadvertently reinforced by rewards. A parent who is quietly waiting out a tantrum is probably doing the right thing. But try to do that at your local supermarket when your child starts screaming for a candy bar, and you're likely to have a stranger tell you that you and your child are both disreputable. Or, even worse, the stranger might just hand your child that candy bar, rewarding the tantrum. Many of us will give into our children's behavior just to get it to stop and to turn off other people's judgment—and that is, of course, the worst thing we can do if we want our children to learn to use their words.

If people out in the world were supportive and understanding, just think of how much better it would be for all of us.

Picture two different versions of an outing:

1. You and your child are at a park. Someone revs a motorcycle loudly on the street nearby. Your child is sensitive to loud

noises, so they scream and put their hands over their ears. Other adults at the park look in your direction, then at each other, shaking their heads. One of them says, loudly enough for you to hear, "There's something wrong with that kid." A couple of parents even station themselves between your child and theirs, as if they're worried your child might harm someone. You feel overwhelmed and ostracized, so you grab your screaming child and head for the car. Your child associates the loud noise with your distress, so their fears about it are reinforced, and they're likely to struggle even more with loud noises in the future. They only have negative associations with the park and are less likely to want to go in the future. And so, frankly, are you.

2. Same initial scenario, except instead of shaking their heads and looking at each other, a couple of the parents smile at you sympathetically. One draws closer and says, "My child hates loud noises, too." Another calls to their own kid, "This friend doesn't like the sound of the motorcycle. What could we do to help distract them?" The child and parent come over and chat with you and try to engage your child until the noise stops and your child calms down. You feel seen, understood, and supported. You end up talking for a longer time to a couple of the parents and you all agree to meet back at the park at some future date. "And don't worry if Sasha gets overwhelmed," one of them says. "We've all been there. No one judges here." You can't wait to come back. And your child has learned that nothing bad happens when there's a loud noise and that the park can be a pleasant place to hang out.

Is that second scenario a foolish dream? Maybe. But we hope not. Don't forget that your child's behavior isn't what changes from one story to the other—that remains the same. It's the way people *react* to that behavior that changes—and what a difference that makes to your child's—and your—ability to socialize and make friends!

Also notice that, in our example, the parents are the ones who need to change the behavior they're modeling. The truth is that children are usually naturally pretty accepting—it's the parents who teach them, either consciously or unconsciously, to be biased. We've dealt with classrooms where the parents complain when a child with autism is included—and meanwhile their kids are perfectly happy to play and engage with the child. And guess what? Students in classes with included children do better! Teachers learn to individualize and implement programs that are better for all the students. So there's no legitimate reason to resent an included child with different needs in the first place. In fact, people who grow up mingling and interacting with kids with differences do better in the workplace, too: no one wants an employee who shows signs of discomfort around a coworker with neurological or physical differences.

If you have a child with any kind of difference, then you're probably already sensitive to other parents' struggles and eager to support and smile at anyone who's dealing with something challenging. But humans should be capable of empathy in situations that they haven't experienced firsthand. Even if your own child is a complete angel (note: no one's child is a complete angel), you should be able to find a well of sympathy inside of you for someone who's trying to teach their child to live in a challenging world, and you should want to teach your own child to be not just a perfect angel behaviorally, but also sympathetic and kind to others.

It doesn't cost anyone anything to smile instead of judge, to offer a hand instead of a cold shoulder, to provide support instead of criticism. Let's all work on this and make the world a more humane and more inclusive place—and one where no one has to behave or look a certain way to be worthy of respect and decency.

Encouraging Empathy Through Education

We've found over time that a lot of people are capable of more empathy than you—or even they—might have thought possible. But before they can tap into those reserves, they often need to be led gently in the right direction.

We once spoke to a high school class where our student, a young man with ASD, was being bullied. We explained the challenges that he faced daily and how hard he was working to be an included member of the classroom.

After we spoke, one of the other students in the class approached us privately. She said she felt horrible because she had been among those teasing our student but had had no idea he was on the spectrum. She regretted being cruel and promised to change her behavior. From then on, she protected and defended our student, and his situation improved drastically.

This is why we highly recommend having a detailed talk about your child with teachers, students, aides, and administrators. Even kindergartners can learn to be more supportive, once they understand a little bit about autism. We urge you to describe not only the challenges your child may face (communication delays, social anxiety, etc.), but also the skills and brilliance your child may not yet have had a chance to show their classmates. They'll see your child as a complete individual, with strengths and weaknesses, and that could lead to a connection they might not have felt before.

This can work with any organized group—scouts, sports teams, religious youth groups, and others. The more you're up-front and informative about your child, with very specific suggestions of what would be helpful, the more you're giving other people a chance to tap into their natural empathy.

It's possible that there's an inherent reason we don't deal well with someone who presents differently—that there's some kind of natural defense mechanism that kicks in when we see something we don't recognize—but that only makes educating people even more important. There was a time when humans thought that anyone who spoke a different language from theirs was speaking gibberish; eventually we learned that every language is equally meaningful, even if we don't understand them all. It's time to get to the same place of respect when it comes to differing behaviors and strengths. And the best way for people to accept someone with differences is for them to see everyone they meet as a complete, rounded, unique human being.

Teaching Socialization

Now that we've been shouting from our soapboxes for a while (note: we need these soapboxes; we're both very short), we'll scramble back down to earth and talk about ways to help your child navigate the outside world, even if the outside world doesn't always live up to our hopes and expectations.

OBSERVE NOW; TEACH LATER.

Don't stress about your child's interrupting behaviors while they're happening out in the world. It may be difficult to see your child's behavior drawing attention, but try to get through the moment without falling apart.

If those behaviors are making socialization difficult, talk with your school, a provider, or someone in the field about strategies for teaching replacement behaviors. You may already have an idea of a replacement behavior and want to start prompting it right away, but make sure you also inform anyone working with or teaching your child, so they can follow through and maintain consistency across all environments. It's much easier to figure out solutions during a quiet time than in a frantic moment.

Also, remember that it isn't a good time to teach if your child is irritated or annoyed. Like any of us, if your child is feeling overwhelmed, they might not absorb new information or even listen. You're likely to be feeling overwhelmed too—it can be stressful when a child engages in interrupting behaviors—so work on staying calm in the moment and taking notes for later. When the crisis has passed, you can work out a teaching plan that can be successfully implemented in small steps over a period of time. Once you've figured out *why* a behavior is interfering with your child's ability to learn or socialize, you can teach a better behavior to replace the undesired one (a process explained in depth in chapter 4, "Tackling Behaviors That Can Dim Your Child's Bright Light"). But, again, wait until you and your child are both calm and able to think clearly before trying to do this, and rope in any experts or team members who might have good ideas.

Consider one parent we know, who brought her son to the neighborhood park, only to find that he was taking the other children's toys for himself. The other kids (and parents) weren't reacting well to this situation, and she knew that if she wanted to continue bringing him to the park, he would have to learn not to take other people's toys. So, she made learning how to share and take turns a goal, one that she worked on at home and asked teachers and specialists to work on as well.

After a few weeks of learning how to take turns and share toys, her son stopped bogarting all the other kids' toys and was able to play appropriately at the park, delighting his mother and increasing his fun.

His mother had taken her time, been thoughtful about her approach, and coordinated the teaching across all of her son's environments—and that's why she succeeded so brilliantly.

USE YOUR TEAM

Remember that you alone are not responsible for figuring all of this out; anyone who supports your child should take a role in figuring out what's impeding the family from going on outings, scheduling playdates, and participating in community events. Reach out to teachers, professionals, and friends for advice and help.

School, with its abundance of potential peers, is a great place to work on anything related to socialization. Teachers should be able and willing to suggest supportive and welcoming classmates and families to get together with outside of school hours.

Unfortunately, we've seen too many IEPs that either don't include social goals or that work on them only with adults. Too often, kids with ASD are left to fend for themselves at recess, with no support at all except for an occasional reprimand from a yard duty supervisor. That's a waste of valuable time with peers, which should be used for teaching socialization.

Children, adolescents, and adults on the autism spectrum report that they yearn for friends and relationships, but if they don't get practice day in and day out like the kids without autism do, they're set up for failure. Please include many social goals in your child's IEP—every child deserves and should have support with socialization (wouldn't that make this a better world?). We've addressed this subject in detail in chapter 5, "Working with Schools to Nurture Your Child's Brilliance."

School isn't the only place children should be getting constant support with socialization. Reach out to providers who offer in-home programs. One elementary schooler was eager to play with other kids at the gathering places in his apartment building, but his in-home provider was only willing to work with him inside his own apartment. His mother changed agencies, and the new one willingly and eagerly provided social support with his peers.

Talk with other parents to find out what would help with playdates, and how to avoid or overcome any potential barriers. Some parents prefer to have playdates at their own house; others send a babysitter, care provider, or service provider when they get invitations; and some children simply go on their own. Figure out what works best for your child and make that happen as often as you can. Try to plan these playdates well in advance—many children have surprisingly busy schedules, so it may be hard to set up a playdate right away, but if you're open to planning ahead, you may be able to get your child on the schedule for a future date.

Your child deserves to socialize (with any necessary support supplied), and peers deserve your child's company.

If you also have a non-autistic child, reach out and offer to have playdates with classmates on the spectrum. It will be great for both kids.

PLAN AHEAD

Planning is important: practicing social areas ahead of time will be helpful for your child. We like to "prime" (practice upcoming activities beforehand), so they're easier and more comfortable in real time. Priming shouldn't be an aversive, drill-type experience: it should be a fun activity, focused on familiarizing your child with areas that may be challenging when first encountered.

You can use priming with any activity—we have several discussions of it in this book in other contexts—but we're going to focus on playdates here. Playdates require both planning an activity and practicing it beforehand.

For example, if there's a plan for your child to bake cookies with a friend, go over the recipe with your child ahead of time, discussing how you measure and add the ingredients, how to shape the cookies, etc. Even better—if you have the time—go ahead and do a test run of making the cookies with your child, so that they're comfortable and have some competence with the activity.

While practicing, you can also suggest things for them to say or to ask their friend. "I like peanut butter—do you?," "My mother doesn't let me eat the batter—does yours?," and so on. A child whose abilities are sometimes hidden out in the world may be relaxed and at their most capable alone with you. Once they've nailed this new accomplishment in this low-stress environment, they'll be more comfortable tackling it again in a less familiar, higher-stakes situation.

One of our students loved the swimming pool at her condominium, but when her mother planned a swimming playdate, the two kids didn't interact in the pool, just swam separately. It didn't really occur to the child that swimming could be social, since she'd always swum alone in the past. After that first playdate, her mother taught her a few pool games, like underwater telephone, Marco Polo, and diving for coins, and the next playdate was much more successful. The pool soon became a favorite way to entertain and interact with peers.

Priming for activities and games makes obvious sense, but priming can also be done for outings and events. We have, for instance, taken many children on field trips before the actual school trip. This allows us to familiarize the child with how the travel will go—whether they'll be on a bus or in a car, and so on—run through what kinds of activities will be expected of them, suggest ways to buddy up with a friend, and propose things they can say and do to engage other students on the trip.

Planning activities and practicing them beforehand make a big difference in performance, confidence, and engagement. Yes, it's more work, but you'll have the satisfaction of seeing your child approaching a social situation with confidence and skills.

KNOW WHAT YOUR CHILD ENJOYS

If necessary, make sure you tweak activities so they're fun for your child and whomever they're playing with. If your sixth-grade child is watching cartoons after school that some parents might not consider age-appropriate, you probably shouldn't show those on a playdate, but knowing how much your kid loves them, you can base an age-appropriate activity around them, like drawing favorite cartoon characters.

If your child gravitates toward books and games that skew young, maybe invite a peer's younger sibling to join on a playdate, so it feels more appropriate to be enjoying those things.

Be creative with what your child enjoys! One child we knew loved to repeat lines from movies, television, and books. Her mother enrolled her in an acting class and then invited classmates to come over and practice lines together.

The goal is to tweak activities that the child with autism already enjoys, so you're making them social, age-appropriate, and entertaining on a playdate for everyone involved.

KEEP PLAYDATES SHORT

We highly recommend keeping playdates short and sweet, especially initially. It's better to have a fun one-hour activity and leave the kids wanting to come back, than try to eke out a four-hour get-together that requires multiple activities and a lot of time that needs to be filled with social conversation, which is likely to be challenging for your autistic child, especially as they get fatigued. Short, well-planned playdates will be less exhausting for you, too.

If there's some distance between your homes, you might want to consider offering to do pick-up and drop-off for these shorter playdates, since some parents may balk at doing a lot of driving for such a short time period.

BEST TIMES AND ACTIVITIES

Look for times, places, and activities when your child is most likely to engage with peers.

One family found that their daughter was most likely to join a social conversation in the car, so the parents drove the carpool every day. That allowed them to encourage their daughter to interact with the other carpool kids in a way that was already comfortable for her. It also gave the parents more control over the situation; they often drove the long way home, to provide her with a few extra minutes to socialize each day. Eventually, with the other parents' permission, they made short stops to extend the social opportunities in ways all the kids could enjoy, like getting ice cream.

If your child has a favorite game or toy at home, send that to school or on a playdate so they'll have a reassuringly familiar activity close at hand to share with a friend. Sometimes we teach the child how to explain the rules of a well-loved game to peers, which adds opportunities for socialization and shows off your child's expertise.

If your child is competent and confident, socialization will be easier, so try to stack the odds in their favor by creating situations where the activity is centered around something they're already skilled at.

And make sure the school is actively fulfilling their part. Too often autistic children are not engaging during free time, breaks, and recess. Ask the school to document how much your child is engaging in these activities that you've already practiced, and what areas need to be targeted. Is your child initiating the play? Explaining the directions? Commenting during the activity? Asking questions? Complimenting? Being a good sport when winning or losing? (This was a huge one for my nephew until we deliberately worked on how to be a good sport.) Sticking with the game until the end? And so on. A coordinated effort, with frequent and consistent supported practice, helps nurture every child's socialization.

EVERY OPPORTUNITY COUNTS

We hate to see any opportunity for socializing wasted. Any teacher or specialist who says things like "Recess is 'free time,' which means all of the children in the class get to choose what they want to do, and your child *chooses* to play alone" should not be teaching. Having friends and relationships is critical for mental health, employment, and engaging in leisure activities in later life, and many students with ASD say they wish they had more friends. So why shrug off the most important social time of the school day?

Socialization needs to be addressed all day long with a consistent and supportive approach.

Lunch time is great for social conversation, yet too often kids are left to fend for themselves, and someone who's socially uncomfortable or hasn't had support in this area may not engage. With just a bit of prompting, a child with ASD can join in the social conversation. This is another place where prompting fun questions might be useful. Also, kids talk a *lot* about food when they're looking at each other's lunches, and food talk is easy to teach because there are so many visual cues. You can teach your kid to ask a classmate if a sandwich tastes good, what they have for dessert, what their favorite cookie is, and so on. You can also stick some interesting facts or pictures in your child's lunch bag to spark topics for social conversation.

If the child needs help opening a container, have the staff direct them to approach a peer, rather than an adult. Don't overlook any opportunity for connection: socialization and social communication improve with practice and feedback. Bring out the best in your child by making sure there are supported opportunities for socialization throughout the day, especially at school where peers can help and support your child—and get to know how talented and smart they really are.

Always remember: verbal autistic adults report that they yearn to have social relationships throughout the life span. Supporting your child in the early years will help them achieve this.

GETTING OUT THERE

Some children just aren't comfortable in new and/or public places. There are a lot of different reasons why this might be: they might not like feeling crowded; they might not like the activity you're there for; they might not like being expected to behave certain ways. And sometimes it's just about the anxiety that any new experience might bring. Here are some suggestions for helping your child enjoy outings more.

1. MAKE OUTINGS FUN. We're not saying you can change their feelings about going places overnight, but a gradual acclimation process with lots of positive rewards will ultimately help your child look forward to going out. For example, if your child hates going grocery shopping with you, try taking them to the store and purchasing one thing that they really like—and nothing else. In and out, with a prize. Repeat this process day after day until they look forward to the outing, and then you can try picking up one or two necessities, followed by another treat. Keep gradually adding things until you can comfortably do your regular shopping with your child (note: this can also be a great time for your child to learn to pay for things, count money, and thank the checker). Any outing can be fun and educational if it's associated with pleasant outcomes.

2. PLAN STRATEGICALLY. One child we worked with became increasingly edgy as the day wore on and fatigue set in, so playdates in the morning or middle of the day were successful, but those in the late afternoon or evening were a disaster. Once the parents figured this out, they were able to schedule playdates early in the day to maximize success. This also speaks to the importance of paying attention to patterns in your child's behavior. In a similar vein, if your child doesn't like sirens, make sure the park you go to is far away from a hospital or fire station. When there are simple solutions, it makes sense to use them.

3. DESENSITIZE YOUR CHILD TO POTENTIAL IRRITANTS. One way to help children with ASD overcome their fears or discomfort is

by exposing them to their cause in a very gradual, controlled, and nonthreatening way. For example, we had one kindergartner who was completely toilet trained. But the loud flush of the industrial toilet at her new school scared her so much, she started to avoid the bathroom and consequently have accidents. The school insisted that she needed diapers, but a closer look revealed the flushing problem. We gradually got her accustomed to the sound of the flush by playing with her a far distance from the bathroom, then very slowly moving closer and closer. Had we not implemented this program, all her successful toilet training would have been lost. (This is another good example of how people can underestimate your child and how you may need to fight to make sure they know how capable your child really is.)

A preschooler we worked with had a major meltdown every time he heard a musical toy. His parents knew that almost every child owns something of the sort, and that made any playdate rife with potential pitfalls. So we worked out a similar desensitization program: we started by turning on a musical toy in another room while engaging the child in enjoyable play and offering him his favorite snacks. Then we gradually moved the toys closer, taking it slow and easy, not rushing it. Pretty soon, the sound of musical toys stopped bothering him, and his family was able to visit friends' homes that they had previously avoided.

Another child couldn't go to school assemblies because the sound of clapping was overwhelming to him. His teacher had instituted a "snapping instead of clapping" rule in the classroom, which was great, but we still needed to work on the issue, since it's pretty clear that an aversion to the sound of applause is going to cut down on a lot of social activities. Fortunately, we were able to gradually help him tolerate clapping by getting him first comfortable with a single clap by one person, then gradually increasing both the number of claps and the number of people clapping, until he was able successfully to attend assemblies and other events. (Quick note: sometimes if a sound bothers a child, it's perfectly acceptable for them to put their hands over their ears. We all hate some loud sounds, so you don't have to rush to work on a relatively minor sound aversion. But if their dislike of a noise has reached a point where it's interfering with socializing or other enjoyable activities, it's time to take steps to tackle the obstacle.)

4. **RELAXING RIGIDITIES.** Some children like things a certain way, which can be fine and even desirable in some situations, but can become a problem when that rigidity gets in the way of socializing and/or learning. One boy we worked with didn't like when anyone else touched his toys. It's hard to have a playdate without sharing toys, so we started getting him used to it by getting duplicate toys, one for each child. The next step was to have him hold the matching toy while watching the other child take a turn playing with the original. Once he was able to watch calmly, we very gradually faded out the second set of toys.

Sometimes children don't understand the idea of "turn taking." In such cases, we start by saying "My turn!" cheerfully, borrowing the toy so very briefly that the child hardly realizes it's gone, then quickly returning it. We very gradually increase how long we keep it on a turn—one second, then two, then three, and so on—until the child can tolerate someone else taking a turn with a toy they've been holding, knowing from experience that they'll eventually get it back.

Other children don't like to see their careful order messed with. One older elementary school boy lined up his toys by size and color and had huge meltdowns when this order was disrupted, which made it hard to have friends visit. So, we modeled laughing and saying, "That's okay!" while moving items he didn't care about. He quickly picked up how to do that, so we started to move items that mattered more to him, and encouraged him to laugh and say "That's okay!" with those, too. He enjoyed the "That's okay!" game and became flexible enough for guests to visit. But we also made sure that the small group of his own items that were *super* special to him were put on a high shelf during playdates, so they wouldn't be disturbed.

Similarly, if my nephew didn't get to open every door before anyone else did, he would get wildly upset and have trouble calming down. Teaching him to take turns worked well to eliminate this problem. We started in a private environment. His dad went first, saying "My turn," and opened the door before Teddy could. At the next door it was "Teddy's turn," and so on. It's surprising how many doors there are to open in a day—the house, the car, the school, the babysitter's, stores . . . Teddy had a lot of turns every day. The first few times it wasn't his turn, he ended up screaming and crying on the floor, but after just a few days of practice, he got the idea that he could still open some doors, just not *every* time.

Children with difficulties being flexible might also respond well to a self-management program. (Please see chapter 4 for a detailed description of this method.) Using self-management, we can teach children to monitor their calmness in these specific situations— something almost anyone could use.

Inflexibilities can interfere with socialization, learning, outings, and many other experiences, so make sure your child can play and interact flexibly.

Fight Back Against Bullying

Individuals diagnosed with autism report higher levels of bullying than their peers do, and teachers confirm this. This can cause long-term mental health issues for children and their families. While we can't take all the mean out of the world, we have had some success with turning bullying around through education. Sometimes people stop being cruel when a situation is explained to them fully, and they're led to a place where they can see a peer as a complete human being and not just a target.

Bullying shows itself in different ways at different stages of life. In early childhood, children may show aggressive or unkind behavior when protecting a toy or sometimes when excluding another child. Physical bullying usually reduces in elementary school and beyond, but cyberbullying, name calling, teasing, excluding, and gossiping are common in older elementary and middle school. Boys are slightly more likely to be physically bullied and girls report more verbal bullying. By high school, bullying drops off a bit but still happens, and can continue in many different forms in the workplace and in social settings outside of school.

Unfortunately, students with learning challenges are often the target of bullying, as are children with social challenges, or any kind of "difference."

Studies report various levels of just how much bullying goes on, but we do know that at least 1 in every 10 kids learns to bully, and the number rises to almost 3 in 10, if all types of bullying are included. We say "learns" to bully because most of the studies distinguish between "intentional" and "unintentional" behavior. For example, if a child accidentally bumps into another in the school hall, that's not intentional. But if a child intentionally bumps into another child, that's bullying. Kids aren't born mean: they develop bullying behaviors if not properly raised, supervised, and instructed. Unfortunately, less than half of children report when they're being bullied, so it can be difficult to get a handle on it while it's happening and provide the needed support.

Bullying is emotionally, socially, and psychologically damaging to children, and, heartbreakingly, at least half of children with ASD report (or their parents or teachers report) being bullied, which is two to three times higher than non-autistic children. And the numbers may be even shockingly higher, depending on the questions studies ask and how the data are collected, and considering the fact that many autistic children may not realize they're being bullied.

You want your child to feel safe in their classroom. It's really the only way they can work at their full potential and reveal all their brilliance. No one who is uncomfortable or feels targeted is going to be able to do their best work.

STEPS WE NEED TO TAKE

We can't be passive about bullying: teachers, staff, families, and students all need to learn awareness of human differences and how to intervene to prevent and stop bullying.

There are ways to combat bullying: working on a student's social skills, setting up peer mediation programs, providing safe classrooms, creating activities and clubs at the school that are based around the student with ASD's interests, and, above all, educating the entire student body about challenges, differences, and neurodiversity.

Increased inclusion, diversity, and targeted education are all needed for school children at any age. Take action at every grade level. Make sure your school is actively and regularly implementing anti-bullying programs and using peer support (which we'll describe below).

Here are some age-specific ways to educate your child's peers about ASD and, in doing so, reduce the likelihood of your child being bullied because of their differences:

1. PRESCHOOL AND YOUNGER. For young children, keep it simple and encourage them to be good helpers. Things like "Mitch is learning how to talk. Do you want to help?" or "Can you help teach Sarah how to take turns?" with instructions and praise will make a huge difference. Young children appreciate adult attention and are usually begging for an opportunity to assist. Take advantage of these natural inclinations and make being a good friend fun for everyone.

2. **ELEMENTARY SCHOOL AGE**. For somewhat older children, we recommend working with teachers to create a presentation that they, you, or someone you trust can give to your child's entire class. This can include examples of differences, an explanation of your child's specific challenges, a description of your child's strengths and talents, and doable ideas for supporting them in the classroom and out. You may be doing this to help your child, but if you're creative and thoughtful in your approach, you're likely to make a positive difference in everyone's life. For example, one parent we know showed the students a can of corn and asked them what was inside. The kids, of course, unanimously agreed that it was corn. The parent then opened it up and showed that it was, in fact, peas (they'd switched the label earlier) and explained that "you can't always tell what's on the inside from the outside." She then went into this concept with humans.

A good message for kids to learn is the idea of trying to help someone who's different rather than making fun of them. Neurodiversity can be a tough thing for kids to understand; in fact, autism has been described as the "invisible" or "hidden" condition. That's why it's especially important to talk to the students about all sorts of differences, including ones they can easily see and understand. By discussing people's need for glasses, crutches, and wheelchairs, you can help children understand that having different needs and requiring some extra support is actually pretty common and doesn't mean the person lacks talent or abilities.

Sometimes we'll ask the class to think of their most challenging subject in school. Math? Writing? History? Everyone has one. Then we'll tell them to think about how it would feel if someone asked them to study that subject all day long. That's how it can feel for autistic children who are expected to talk and socialize all day.

Again, once students have some context and empathy for their fellow student with ASD, we like to provide them with specific examples of how they can offer support. Children can help with prompting communication, playing games, interacting at recess, having playdates, and so on. Be specific, model how to help, and provide positive feedback to the peers, and important bonds will develop and strengthen.

3. **MIDDLE SCHOOL AND HIGH SCHOOL AGE.** Here's where you can scale up both the size and scope of your presentation. For instance, one school allowed us to present at an assembly of the entire eighth-grade class. We detailed the characteristics of ASD and put our student's challenges with making friends into that context, so the children understood there was a logical basis to their peer's difficulties. We also discussed how they would all feel if they weren't included in activities or invited places. The very next day, our student's father reported that, for the first time ever, three classmates greeted him at drop-off, and within a week he had been invited to several hangouts outside of school.

We also like to detail the student's strengths at these presentations and ask the classmates for how to include the student more, specifically using these skills.

We've done many of these presentations and have been consistently pleased with their outcomes. Educating people on neurodiversity makes a difference. And if you don't feel comfortable doing the education yourself, reach out to the school, another professional, or a friend to help.

Please note that some parents or professionals choose not to have the student with ASD in the room during the presentation. There are pros and cons to that choice: it can sometimes provide a more open forum for questions and discussion if the child is absent, but they may feel left out and/or uncomfortable knowing that this is happening without them. If the child with ASD is included and verbal, they may be able to explain what they find challenging.

Again, the peers are likely to respond to a feeling of personal connection and a description of specific goals. They don't always notice when a child is struggling socially and may not be able to come up with helpful ideas without support. So be specific, provide feedback, and lavish praise for kind, caring, and helpful actions.

THE INHERENT DESIRE TO HELP

No matter what their age, kids love to be given responsibility and then be recognized for their helpfulness. You might be surprised how many other students already have relatives or family friends with ASD and are predisposed to be helpful—they just need some guidance. Give them purpose by having them lend a hand to support your child's social development and engagement. Describe, illustrate, and communicate your child's strengths.

One child was a whiz at calendar calculations, and once this was known, every child came running to find out what day of the week they were born on. Another student was great at puzzles (and could even do them upside down); putting puzzles on the lunch table for a group activity meant his peers could see and admire this skill.

Describing a student's likes and dislikes allows their classmates to keep an eye out for them—for example, "Jerry loves to swing and watch videos, but is overwhelmed by loud noises and dogs"—and to come up with ideas to expand on the likes and avoid the dislikes.

Educating classmates about your child's strengths, hidden talents, and preferences can change a course of thought from a lack of comprehension to recognition of your child as a valuable and appreciated classmate.

SEEK OUT PEERS IN NATURAL SETTINGS

Commit these words to memory: peer-mediated support (PMS), which is also referred to as peer-mediated interventions (PMI) in the literature. We want you to ask for this at your child's next IEP. Refer back to chapter 5, "Working with Schools to Nurture Your Child's Brilliance," for more details on this. We do go into the subject at great length there, but we'll include an overview here as well, since we find it to be such a vital and meaningful part of any child's social growth.

Peers can be terrific helpers if they're properly trained and educated: they can provide ongoing support in the natural environment, they can pick out areas that are important to kids that adults might not even have considered, and they can form bonds with your child that reach far beyond expectations. Enlisting peers is also time- and cost-efficient: they're always available, unlike skilled (and often expensive) specialists. Finally, peers interact differently than adults, who can't really mimic the natural interactions that a child is likely to face in the classroom and out in the yard.

For all these reasons, recruiting peers to help and support a child with ASD is vital for the most positive long-term outcomes, no matter what your child's present verbal or social level is.

Socializing can be practiced in one-on-one or small group settings, but research shows that these usually don't generalize to natural settings, which is a huge flaw. It's clear that at least some of the social learning needs to take place in a natural setting, a place where kids play together already. This part is too often missing.

Peer mediation isn't as simple as telling the kids they should all play together. We all know that's unlikely to happen on its own. PMI needs to be systematically developed, systematically implemented, and systematically monitored.

Here are some tips for creating a successful PMI program.

1. AT SCHOOL, RECRUIT AN ENTIRE PEER CLIQUE RATHER THAN AN INDIVIDUAL PEER. Research shows that enlisting an entire clique leads to longer involvement and increases the likelihood that the group will include your child in outings outside of the designated peer mediation period.

2. **CHOOSE THE PEERS YOU RECRUIT CAREFULLY.** While many may volunteer to help out, stick to the ones who already have something in common with your child and, if possible, already get along with them. Also, consider the personality of the volunteers: some studies show that children differ in their abilities to get a job done (some help too much or too little), and you want to find the ones with the perseverance and interest to keep going, even if it's not always easy.

3. **TRAIN THE PEERS WITH EXPLICIT INSTRUCTIONS AND REGULAR FEEDBACK.** We find that role-playing is a great way to help the peers figure out how to support the child with ASD in a variety of different possible scenarios. For example, if the child with autism doesn't want to share a toy, how might a peer intercede? The most common probabilities can be addressed in role play and re-addressed during regular meetings. Some peers will need more support than others.

   We visited a high school in Los Angeles where the incredible SLP had arranged an active lunchtime group for the students with social needs (this doesn't happen often, but it should). Right after eating, the recruited peer mediators located the students they had been paired with and started to help them reach out socially, using approaches they'd been taught in previous instructions that were tailored to each specific child. It was wonderful to see all the connections being made. With peer mediation, specific goal areas are taught to the peer, the peer is observed in real time, and then provided with feedback and suggestions.

4. **INSTITUTE REGULAR MEETINGS WITH THE PEER GROUP TO REVIEW HOW THINGS ARE GOING, AND TO OFFER FEEDBACK, EXTRA GUIDANCE, AND SUGGESTIONS.** Whether or not the child with ASD is included in these meetings is up to the discretion of the staff involved. The same person running the meetings should also be observing the

peer interactions out in the field where they're occurring. This is the best way to note any issues that might be cropping up and to think strategically about ways to improve them.

5. REMEMBER: ADULTS INTERACT DIFFERENTLY THAN PEERS DO, SO IT'S REALLY IMPORTANT TO SEE HOW KIDS THE SAME AGE AS YOURS ARE SOCIALIZING, IN ORDER TO HELP YOUR CHILD GAIN THE SKILLS TO NAVIGATE APPROPRIATELY. For instance, in the field, we've noticed that peers do a lot of playful teasing during a game. An adult might say, "Good game" or "Good roll," but a peer is far more likely to say something along the lines of "You blew it!" or "I won!" Once you're aware of this kind of thing, you can make sure the child with ASD is exposed to gentle teasing in a way that allows them to learn how to cope with it and be a good sport (or at least as good a sport as kids tend to be about these things).

OLDER STUDENTS CAN HELP, TOO

As students get older, they tend to need community service hours: recruiting a high schooler to help at a middle school can be cool for the younger autistic student. Similarly, an older elementary student may be helpful with a younger one. Whether the student is the same age or older, training, feedback, and rewarding their efforts will always lead to the greatest success and longevity.

One school helped us recruit a group of fifth graders to play ball with Jackson, a nonverbal first grader. Although the program was asking them to help him only during lunch recess, this group waited outside his classroom before every lunch, recess, or assembly, took him under their wings, brought in their own balls from home, and supported him in every way possible. Their engagement with Jackson went far beyond the peer lunchtime activity *we* had arranged.

MAKE USE OF YOUR CHILD'S INTERESTS AND TALENTS

We know your child has unique interests, talents, and strengths. If they don't seem as interested in socializing as you'd like, try to set up formal opportunities based on these skills and passions. Sometimes it's easier to get the other kids interested in what your child loves rather than the other way around. We've had preschoolers who only wanted to open and close doors, so we recruited other kids to take turns doing just that. This also gave us an opportunity to teach about how hinges work and how doors are mounted—something little ones find interesting.

We have developed clubs from scratch specifically for our students with an intense interest in a single subject. The great thing about this is that the student usually has more knowledge and competence in the area than anyone else, so they can easily earn their peers' respect and admiration, and clubs can be created for any age group.

Even if it feels like your child's skills and knowledge won't translate to a school activity, you can often figure something out with a bit of creativity. We had one student who loved movies, which she watched at home with her family. Watching the movies wasn't doable at school, but we were able to develop a "famous lines and famous actors" game to play at recess, and she was always a sought-after team member because of her wealth of information. Of course, she delighted in the game, since it was all about a subject that interested her. Socialization should always, first and foremost, be fun for everyone involved.

Adults with autism can sometimes find clubs or activities in the community that speak to their interests, but it's helpful to send a support person who's close in age, at least initially. Our adults have enjoyed participating in meet-up groups focused on hiking, walking, history, photography, dancing, tennis, and many other activities. Once there's a good comfort level, the support person can fade off.

Hosting Special Events

Since we're talking about creating social opportunities based around your child's skills and interests, let's consider what you can do at home.

Theme parties are fun for everyone—who doesn't love to be invited to a party? One child we worked with knew a ton about the U.S. presidents, so his family threw a Presidents' Day party. The big moment—totally impressive to all his peers—was when he stood up and recited all the presidents in order.

Another child, who loved baking, hosted a cupcake-decorating party. Since this was a skill she had already mastered, she was able to show her peers how to make perfect frosting flowers, swirls, leaves, and rainbows. Her skill impressed everyone, and they all completely enjoyed the activity.

Many people on the spectrum are extremely talented artists and musicians; having an art show or concert can be a great way to show off these talents. One family created an art gallery in their home, complete with easels to display their child's colorful paintings. They put out food and drinks, so people could wander around the house, enjoying the artwork and chatting—and even buy a painting, if they wanted to bring one home. Everyone wanted to talk to the artist, to compliment his work, and ask about his methods and materials, and he chattered away, thrilled to be discussing something he excelled at.

Events like these can be specially designed to showcase your child's talents in the comfort of your own home. And if your child needs to have some private time, which many people do during intense social events, they can slip away to a bedroom for a few minutes and recharge.

Since it's your home, you can control the situation and make sure that everything about the event feels comfortable for your child: the length, the location, the guests, and the focus.

Socialization is important for long-term quality of life and should be encouraged, arranged, and supported regularly. Getting started with a well-planned program and some creative ideas will help fulfill your child's desire to be a part of their peer group, and the peers will have an opportunity to get to know your wonderful child's strengths.

Online Socializing

These days most kids spend a lot of time using screens for entertainment, socializing, shopping, and communicating. You want to make sure your child isn't spending an excessive time alone with a screen, playing video games or engaging in other solitary pursuits. If you find that's the case, think about ways to replace that behavior with something equally enjoyable but more social.

If your child is lonely and clinging to electronic games for entertainment, it's essential to make these games more social and/or to help your child find other social activities that they'll enjoy that can replace the alone time.

For instance, Costa loved playing video games by himself, so his parents invited his friends, who were also interested in electronics, to hang out with him after school and play video games together. Even though Costa was still playing electronic games, he was also constantly interacting with his friends, since they chatted while they played. A planned snack break offered them the opportunity to step away from the monitors and discuss the games further. Video games were no longer a solitary pursuit for Costa, but an important part of an active social life. And his friends' parents were equally delighted to know that their kids were connecting with others and not just in their rooms playing alone. (It's a fairly common problem for all young people, not just autistic ones.)

Dave's absorption in the internet verged on addiction. He got upset when his parents asked him to leave the computer to do homework, help with a household chore, or play a game, and he expressed no interest in having a peer hang out with him. Concerned, his parents gradually began enrolling him in after-school classes, in subjects he enjoyed and was happy to learn more about.

In addition, realizing his attention was easier to capture before he sat down at the computer than once he was already deep into it, they created a list of chores he was required to finish before he could even turn on the computer. They started with just one chore and gradually added more, so he could get used to the idea without feeling overwhelmed.

BONDING OVER SHARED INTERESTS

One interesting thing to think about is helping your child connect to people with similar interests through the internet. Sometimes a child with ASD has such huge knowledge of one subject that they can't find people who can keep up with them at home or school. While you definitely want to monitor extensive engagement with strangers, we do know of several kids who made lifelong friends through online blogs and forums that focused on their esoteric interests.

One young man, for example, loved fantasy and science-fiction novels and movies. He found an online group of people with a similar deep knowledge of the genre and had such passionate discussions with them that they often continued in private messages. Later, with his parents' supervision and involvement, he met and became friends in real life with one of his favorite fellow group members. And a high schooler, who loved birdwatching but found that other people her age tended to laugh when she mentioned it, found a small online group of high school birdwatchers and, with her parent's supervision, began bird watching with them.

SOCIAL MEDIA

If your child chooses to engage on social media, they may need some support on what to post, how to word messages, and when internet relationships should be avoided. Ground rules about who they may

follow, friend, and correspond with should be clear, and some children may need regular supervision while on social media.

Here are some examples of simple and supportive ways families
helped when someone with ASD struggled a bit with social media:

- High school student Janis was a great artist who liked to post
  drawings on Instagram of cartoon characters that appeal to
  younger children. Her sister helped her curate her online art to
  make it more age appropriate, and soon her schoolmates invited
  her to join the art club.

- Ian's peer mediator helped him compose more appropriate
  messages after Ian sent a few texts that were too direct and
  friends viewed as hurtful. With a bit of direction, Ian learned to
  soften his responses and connect better with his peers.

- Liz's parents put a parental control on a dating app when they
  found she was conversing with someone who was almost four
  times her age.

- Adam's social communication differences made it difficult
  for him to engage with other children at family parties, so his
  parents let him watch YouTube videos during get-togethers.
  When we placed a vibrating watch on his wrist and taught him
  to point out what he was watching whenever it vibrated (e.g.,
  "Look at this funny dog video!"), his viewing became a way to
  connect socially and pull others in.

- Phil's parents noticed he was spending so much time on online
  coding sites that it was cutting back on his socializing. So they
  enrolled him in a coding class, where he became the star student.

High internet usage is associated with inattention, poorer grades,
and decreased relationships with peers, and children and adolescents

with ASD spend more time than those without playing solitary video games. If you find that your child is spending too much time surfing the web, playing video games, or doing other online activities that aren't social and don't involve homework, it's time to start looking for appealing social activities. You don't have to pull the plug in one day—that may be too jarring—just take note and work to gradually decrease solitary time. Increase other desirable activities, find computer activities that are social, and make clear, easy-to-follow rules about when your child can go online and what they're allowed to do on there. Your child will be a lot better off in the long run.

You don't need to tackle this alone. Your child's school has undoubtedly dealt with this issue in the past and should have some good advice and suggestions for you. A home program can also be invaluable for setting up guidelines and working with your child to replace too much alone time with social activities that will improve their quality of life.

SUMMARY

Having friendships is a meaningful part of life, but the communication challenges of ASD can make establishing those early connections difficult for your child, so we all need to put in the work to make them happen. You may have to think deeply about the best ways to make socializing fun for your child, but we promise you that you'll find something. Even children with limited communication skills can play games with no rules, just turn-taking. Ask at your local toy store for help finding a game that will intrigue and engage your child. Be patient when you teach game-playing skills. It may be hard for your child to let someone else take a turn initially, so teach turn-taking gradually, as we described earlier in the chapter. Games with no winners or losers might be a great place to start.

Children with strong language skills can pick out age-appropriate games that appeal to them. You can help them learn how to play them and, once they're comfortable, send those games to school to play with peers.

Find out what your child naturally gravitates toward doing at their school and then work with the staff to incorporate social interactions into those activities. For example, if your child goes to the library each lunch period, have the school start a book club. If your adolescent likes drawing comics, start a comic book club. If your college student likes anime, search for an anime club on campus or in the community. There are countless clubs out in the world, so one is likely to fit your child's age and interests, but if you can't find one, see if you can create one.

As often as possible, redirect your child to ask peers for items, help, information, advice, and support. Make sure the school has active peer-mediation programs. We all need to support one another, and peers are the perfect resource, always there, usually eager to help, and often quick to learn.

Providing your child with tools for effective socialization will set them on the path toward long-lasting friendships and relationships.

CHAPTER 8

Finding the Joy and Holding On to It

There may be times when knowing that your child is way more amazing, brilliant, and wonderful than the world seems to notice or acknowledge feels overwhelming to you. You see evidence of your child's depth of understanding and empathy every day, but sometimes it feels like all people want to do is point out their struggles and challenges.

That kind of frustration can be extremely stressful, as can the fact that, although many children have wonderful outcomes, some diagnosticians will give unnecessarily worrisome prognoses.

Professionals have no right to paint a dark, scary portrait of your child's future. No one has a crystal ball, and, for a child with ASD, a positive and supportive attitude combined with the right program can lead to wide-open possibilities. Don't scare yourself with too many internet searches that focus on the challenges of autism, or with books that paint autism as a devastating tragedy, or with movies and novels that overdramatize the sorrows of being autistic. Science is discovering new approaches daily, and acceptance is higher than ever, giving your child many more opportunities than they might have had just a few decades ago.

We want you to avoid any downward spirals and to be the best parent you can for your amazing child—and to enjoy them (and any other children you might have) as much as you can. This may require a conscious effort to change the way you think and act, to learn to be comfortable reaching out to family and friends, and to tap into available community resources, so that you have support and breaks without spending all of your hard-earned cash.

Family Cohesion

We know that getting an ASD diagnosis can be stressful, but we're happy to report that research shows that families who stick together after an ASD diagnosis often have a stronger and more meaningful bond than they did before. When a family works together as a unit, stress and depression are lessened. For some families, all of this pulling together comes naturally; others need to make a thoughtful effort to divide responsibilities and forge a path to mutual respect.

At the risk of oversimplification, here's a bullet list of some steps you can take to help your family grow closer while supporting a child with ASD:

- FIGURE OUT WHAT'S CAUSING DISCOMFORT AND TARGET THAT DIRECTLY. Getting professional help if someone in the family is struggling emotionally is like seeing a doctor when you have pneumonia: it's a wise and necessary thing to do to get and stay healthy and strong. Staying ahead of breakdowns and implosions is the best way to avoid them altogether.

- LEARN TO COMPLIMENT YOUR PARTNER(S) FOR EVERY SMALL THING THEY DO AND TO SUPPORT THEM WHEN THEY'RE STRUGGLING. Positive reinforcement works for all of us: we naturally increase behaviors that make us feel good and decrease those that make us feel bad. Every time a family member notices and compliments an effort we've made, it makes us want to keep trying and helps us appreciate that we're part of a team.

- **COORDINATE WITH YOUR PARTNER(S) IN POSITIVE WAYS.** Don't criticize if you think other family members aren't implementing goals correctly or as often as you'd like (let a professional help with that). Positive suggestions and demonstrating a successful approach will go a lot further than criticism.

- **WORK ON YOUR RELATIONSHIP.** All children pick up on family conflict, which can create yet another cyclical problem: the anxious child might fall apart, which makes the family members more tense, which makes them turn on each other, which then makes the child more anxious. If you're finding that stress is making you irritable with your partner(s), examine that behavior and, if necessary, seek out support to reduce it.

Become Educated

Learning to implement and follow through with teaching strategies isn't a luxury—it's a necessity. The literature is quite clear that children learn fastest when there's a consistent approach: they'll have greater generalization of gains across settings, and their newly learned behaviors will be more durable.

When you learn techniques to help your child communicate and interact successfully with others, it boosts your sense of worth and competency, leading to a reduction of stress. On the other hand, not knowing what to do in a situation lowers self-esteem and increases feelings of guilt, both of which *increase* stress. Learning the correct ways to teach, guide, and interact with your child will reverse that course, and you'll learn those through parent education, which should be offered by the professionals you work with. You can also educate yourself by reading and attending conferences and symposiums (most offer online options, so you don't have to travel).

Of course, there are different types of parent education programs, and some are better than others. Regrettably, some will actually increase stress. No one should expect a parent to become their child's therapist: your interactions need to take place within the context of your daily, familial, loving, and undoubtedly busy life. If someone is expecting you to set up a classroom in your own home and drill your child, reject that approach and find something comfortable and fun for your child and for you. All children learn life skills by watching and helping their parents, and goals can and should be implemented in this context of daily routines. Spend time with your child and make the most of everyday learning opportunities.

For example, if your child loves to go outside and you're working on language skills, you can encourage them to say "Open!" before you open the door. If you're setting the table, have your child help with that task, making it clear that a set table leads to a tasty meal (a natural reinforcer!), and that they're a crucial, productive, and valued member of the family. Their ability to help and their pride in helping will lower stress for both of you.

The right kind of parent education will make you aware of many more similar opportunities that will arise during your days together.

Reframe the Way You're Thinking About Your Child

You should never simply say "Be happy!" to someone who isn't—it can become one more item on the to-do list or, even worse, one more thing they feel like they're failing at.

But sometimes we do fall into negative ways of looking at things, and it's worth being thoughtful about our own attitudes, so we can find our way back to appreciating the positives in our lives. We all have the ability to reshape the patterns our neural pathways fall into, and if you're feeling like your thoughts just keep going down a dark path, it might be worth making an effort to send them in a different direction.

Here are some suggestions for doing that:

1. **TRY TO STAY AWAY FROM ANY KIND OF SELF-BLAME.** Parents have a tendency to blame themselves for every struggle their child goes through. But if you're supporting and loving your child to the best of your abilities, try to let go of the guilt and self-blame. You're a loving, caring parent. That's what matters.

2. **FOCUS ON TAKING STEPS THAT ARE PRODUCTIVE.** As we said earlier, if you're actively helping your child learn, and you're seeking out additional people you trust to help them overcome challenges, you'll feel better about your role in their life. Feeling incapable and inactive is enervating, while feeling capable and active is invigorating.

3. **APPRECIATE EVERY SUCCESS.** It's important to have long-term goals for your children and yourself, but also try to make sure that you and the professionals you work with are setting goals that are small enough to achieve, so that everyone experiences regular success. Feeling capable of supporting your child's unique needs will build up your confidence, which will help both you and your child. Nothing succeeds like success—and a lot of small successes lead in time to big gains. If the school only reports to you when there's a problem, ask them to report—ideally every single school day—an area where your child succeeded. This won't just make *you* feel better; it will change the way both the school and your entire family look at your child. Similarly, take note of every success at home and share it with others. You know your child is amazing: tell the world.

4. **ACCEPT AND REVEL IN THE WAYS YOUR CHILD IS UNIQUE.** Always, always, always focus on the amazing things that your child does

that are exciting and interesting and unique. Use these fascinating talents to engage and encourage them.

5. **DON'T FRET ABOUT SMALL BEHAVIORS OR SCARE YOURSELF ABOUT THE FUTURE.** Stay focused on supporting your child in ways that will benefit them—helping them to communicate and socialize—and shrug off the small stuff, like "stimming" behaviors (rocking, repetitive hand motions, etc.) or a lack of eye contact and/or joint attention. These smaller things often fall into place without needing to be taught directly, when your child's motivation improves during social communication. Worried they may affect your child's success in the future? Maybe this will help: we have a brilliant friend who's a professor with ASD. He exhibits stims during his lectures, and guess what? His students adore him and frequently nominate him for professor of the year! (He's also married with two wonderful children.)

Getting Ahead of Interfering Behaviors

Most parents will try to avoid a place or situation where their child routinely falls apart, even if it means they're missing out on something they might enjoy. While it helps to know that most behaviors have a communicative function, as we've discussed earlier in this book, knowledge alone might not eliminate the discomfort of being out in public with a child who's having meltdowns. But it's not fair to your child—or to you—to avoid community activities that have the potential to be enjoyable and meaningful, so take your time, stay the course, identify the behavior's communicative function, and address it appropriately and promptly. There's a good chance you'll find a successful way to navigate being out in the world, and both you and your child will be the happier for it.

As we've discussed in previous chapters, try to stay calm when your child is having a meltdown, even if it's in public. It's difficult, if not impossible, to teach in the middle of a crisis moment, so don't even try. Just take notes on what might have triggered the meltdown (mental notes are fine, and remember it's not always about what just happened; sometimes it's about what your child would *like* to have happen but can't communicate appropriately), develop a plan for teaching replacement behaviors, and begin implementing it across all settings when things are calmer and your child is open to learning.

Taking your time to do this right may mean that, for a while, you have to ask for help, educate people, and ignore anyone who wants to judge you or your child. (Easier said than done, but we promise that, if you're working on long-term improvement rather than reacting in the moment, you're doing this right.)

Let anyone who works with your child know that there's a behavior that needs to be reduced. They might not see your child out in the world, so they might not be aware of these disruptions.

In chapter 3, "Communication: The Bridge That Connects," we provided detail on how to help your child successfully communicate their needs and wants to reduce meltdowns and other interfering behaviors. Always remember that all children need to learn communicative behaviors to replace the inappropriate ones. Effective communication may be a sign, a signal, a word, or a sentence. The important thing is that your child make an attempt to communicate with you.

Without an alternative way to communicate, the crying, meltdowns, and aggression will return, even if you've worked to reduce them. Teaching a different way to communicate will steadily decrease the behaviors that make outings challenging. Sometimes these behaviors need to be taught and practiced in more controlled settings before you plunge into a community outing. It can be difficult to focus on teaching skills when you're out running errands or attending an event, so practicing at home makes sense. Luckily, there are many important social behaviors (like learning to take turns, wait patiently, ask nicely for a treat, or respond appropriately when a toy is taken away) that can easily be practiced in a controlled, private setting.

Rewards can sometimes make a big difference to a child who's struggling to hold it together, as we've discussed in our "self-management" section. You might want to assemble a special bag of cherished toys or activities that are available only at certain special times, like during a long, unpleasant wait at the doctor's office or once your child has managed a successful transition back to the car after having to leave a highly desired activity.

Always remember that you and your child have just as much right to participate in community activities as anyone else, and the only way your child is going to learn the expectations of that setting is through participation. Support your child as you both figure out the best ways to navigate being out in the world. Over time you'll reap the benefits of being able to do more and more with them, rather than less and less.

Fighting Back Against Financial Strain

Skilled support can be incredibly expensive. Even if insurance helps out, there are still those nasty co-pays. Most cost analyses have shown that specialized programs are essential to a more favorable long-term outcome, so parents rightly try to figure out how to afford them, but that can lead to stressful levels of economizing while still watching bank accounts dwindle.

Along with these costs, parents may wish to secure a more experienced child care provider—someone who understands and can deal with the communication and behavioral differences—rather than a local neighborhood babysitter. That extra experience and training can be expensive, too.

If you're feeling financial strain, there are some ways to find relief. First, many insurance companies charge a co-pay each time the provider visits. Often you can arrange for fewer visits that last for longer time periods, avoiding multiple co-pays.

Many local organizations will help with finances for your child's treatment; reach out to charitable organizations, nonprofits, and clubs for help. Similarly, search for appropriate grants and other state programs. Some will cover direct expenses related to your child, and others will help out with indirect expenses, like replacing a broken washing machine. Many states have programs that will cover direct services, such as child care, respite care (i.e., a covered break for the primary caregiver), and transportation. Some programs even cover a "helper" to assist with things like laundry, errands, and cleaning.

Another source of support are nonprofits that offer classes free to individuals with differences. We've seen everything from dance to surfing to social skills being taught completely free to those with documented "disabilities." (We recommend looking for these even if money isn't an issue for you. They can be fun for your child and give you both something to look forward to.)

If you live near a university, many of them run studies offering state-of-the-art programs that your child can participate in for free; some even will offer a financial incentive, such as reimbursement for gas or a stipend for your participation. There are also graduate training programs that offer children with autism supervised services, so the graduate students can earn practicum units toward graduation.

Some universities require that incoming graduate students have personal experience with a family, so that they understand the day-to-day issues many experience. And some colleges that offer undergraduate courses in autism can help you find students who would like to get experience in the field by providing supervision and child care. If your local college or university says they don't have a system in place to connect students and families, help them develop these opportunities. Students living away from their families may greatly appreciate the opportunity to get out of their dorms and spend time in a warm family home.

Many professionals provide some pro bono work each month,

so ask if you need it. In fact, ask for discounts for everything if you need them—books, conferences, online courses, etc. You might be surprised how often you can get a discount if you have a justifiable reason for asking for one.

Try to be creative with child care solutions. We know two couples, both with autistic children, who trade off Saturday night child care, so they can take turns going out. You may be able to find some highly motivated and thoughtful high school students willing to babysit, who need community service hours, and would be excited to learn procedures for working with children with ASD. We've worked with a lot of responsible, reliable, and intelligent high schoolers who, with training, supported our families just as well as—or even better than—some of the professional service providers. Reach out to your local high schools to see if they can pass your information on to interested students. You or one of your service providers can train the high schooler until you're comfortable that they're ready to be alone with your child. (You can always test this out by staying at home the first time, in another room, if you're nervous.)

Online programs in an appealing subject might be another good, free option for a child who can sit in front of the computer. We prefer the ones that have some social interaction built in. There are free classes in many areas of interest, and many have live instructors. If your child finds a topic fascinating, it's a great way to get a break for yourself while helping them stay engaged and stimulated.

It's worth shaking a few trees to uncover some helpful support out there. There really are systems in place to help support those struggling to pay for the services they need.

Collaborate and Communicate

A system of collaboration and communication with specialists, teachers, and staff is important for a child's success—and for a parent's peace of mind. Please don't wait until there are problems to reach out to a school or program: it's far more helpful to communicate regularly from the very beginning. We recommend a daily written log that passes back and forth (virtually or physically) between the home and other environments, so everyone can be literally on the same page.

And while you're sharing information, ask for your team to include photos or short video clips of your child whenever possible. It's encouraging to see snapshots or videos of successes, and it can be helpful and meaningful to also view the challenges that crop up in other environments, so everyone can get to work on them.

We also encourage regular team meetings, which help remind everyone of the goals you're working toward and provide an opportunity to discuss which approaches are effective and which are not. The *team* in teamwork stays closer and more collaborative if everyone is meeting regularly.

Please see chapter 5, "Working with Schools to Nurture Your Child's Brilliance," for more on working with your school and professionals to make sure your child is getting consistency across every setting.

Meeting Sleep Needs

Some children with ASD experience more sleep difficulties than their peers do, which almost always means less sleep for their parents. And we don't need research to tell us that sleep deprivation leads to challenges in other areas. We've all learned that through experience (unless you're someone who has never tossed and turned all night long, in which case, we salute you and would like you to tell us your secret!).

While some sleep issues may be behavioral (e.g., a child has learned to depend on someone else to help them get to sleep or is taking too many naps), others may be biological. Some kids simply need less sleep than others. Fortunately, either way, there are behavioral strategies that can help everyone get more rest.

First, keep a log of your child's sleeping, 24/7, for long enough to spot any patterns.

One older elementary school student we worked with was being allowed to sleep for hours in school each day and, needless to say, wasn't the least bit drowsy at bedtime. Identifying the school naps as the issue and eliminating them fixed the problem. Another child took a bus to a school all the way across town, and the naps he took on the bus were just enough to assure that he wasn't tired at night.

If your child is sleeping during the day but not at night, and has passed the age where naps are recommended, make sure that you help them stay awake all day long—encourage them to walk, play, wash their face, etc., if they start to feel drowsy. We want fatigue to set in at night, when you need them to sleep, so *you* can.

For children who simply don't need a lot of sleep, you can teach them to stay in their rooms and not wake up any other family members until it gets light outside or they recognize a certain time on the clock. They may not get any more sleep themselves, but the rest of you will.

This is yet another time where your knowledge of your child's interests and skills comes in handy. Does your child gravitate toward timetables and clocks? Then you can find a clock your child likes to look at and mark where the little hand needs to be before they can wake you up, or have the time written out next to a digital clock and teach them it has to "match" before they can wake you. If your child loves nature and/or is a visual learner, then maybe it's about when the sun comes up and hits a certain spot in their room. Be creative and think about ways your child might learn best what time is "waking-up time."

Reducing liquid consumption in the evening can be helpful if you've noticed your child is getting up to use the bathroom or waking up after accidents at night.

Creating regular routines around bedtime and sleep tends to improve sleep overall: once you have a good bedtime routine you all enjoy, stick with it, and try to make it happen at the same time every day.

If a child doesn't like to be left alone at bedtime, it might help to find a cuddly toy that they can cling to. Another option some parents find useful is to allow their kids to get up during the night and come into their rooms, so long as they don't wake their parents up. They can lie down on a sleeping bag or sofa and go back to sleep there. While you don't want to encourage dependence, sometimes a compromise like this is the best way to keep everyone sleeping as much as possible.

You can also help your child gradually learn to feel comfortable sleeping independently. One parent, who slept with her fifth grader every night, put a cot in her child's room and slowly moved it farther and farther away over the course of a month, until he could tolerate her being out of his room at night.

Getting a good night's sleep will help you feel energetic and is equally good for your child's development. There are lots of ways to improve your child's sleep and, if you're feeling stuck, there are professionals who can help with this.

Food Aversions

Many children with ASD have food aversions, which can make mealtimes complicated for whoever does the household cooking. But only serving foods that the child recognizes and already likes can also cause a parent anxiety, since a severely restricted diet is rarely a fully nourishing one. We want to keep our kids both happy with their food choices *and* well nourished, and it's stressful to feel like we're constantly choosing between these two options. Besides, you can't expand a restricted diet if you never offer new foods, and you want to improve the situation over time.

If your child has a restricted diet that's making it hard to plan family meals or go out to eat, we recommend desensitizing the child to new tastes and textures. We like to start by having the child simply hold a new food in their hand; then, once they're comfortable with that, touch it to their lips, then the tongue, then take a tiny bite (it's okay to spit it out at first), then chew, then chew and swallow. None of this is painful to the child—it's slow, gentle, and accommodating—and many of the children end up liking the new foods they try. We recently got a call from a mom, who had just tried this gentle approach with her favorite food, tuna, and was thrilled and pleased that her initially averse son had finally eaten some—and liked it!

It's always a good idea to keep introducing foods into the rotation, even if your child isn't interested at first; studies have shown that it can take as many as twenty repeated exposures to a new food before a child is willing to try it. Take it slowly and in baby steps. That's a lot easier for everyone and you're more likely to experience success in the end.

We've also found that slight variations in the restricted foods can be helpful: for instance, if your child is willing to eat regular French fries, try ordering different kinds of fries, like sweet potato or garlic-parmesan, and then expand to other potato dishes. Your child might be more open to new tastes in familiar shapes. For older children, adolescents, or adults, you can look through menus with them and ask them to pick out foods they're willing to eat—the fun of choosing for themselves may lead them to find something you might not have thought they'd want. And many restaurants are willing to make substitutions or changes on orders—we knew one child who would order "A cheeseburger—hold the beef!"

Similarly, taking adolescents and older picky eaters to the grocery store may help them find new foods to try; let them pick out anything they want, so long as it's healthful and they haven't had it before. One family that tried this reported that after months of these grocery excursions, their son was able to travel to other countries and eat all new foods without any issues.

There are many ways to use your child's interests and knowledge to increase the foods they're willing to eat. If they love a certain book, see if it mentions any food in it. We know one child who thought he hated vegetables, but he loved the Redwall novels and was willing and even eager to try any of the dishes the vegetarian mice ate in the books. If your child is interested in trains, look up what kinds of restaurants have stands in different train stations and build off of that; someone who likes art might respond to still-life paintings with food and be willing to try something they see there. Again, making use of your child's interests can lead to success.

Expanding the food repertoire will increase the number of restaurants you can eat at, allow you to visit friends more easily, and reduce the need for you to cook or carry the few foods your child enjoys. And of course, a well-rounded diet makes for better nutrition. Just keep the introductions slow and steady, and you'll see progress.

Self-Help Skills

Many children with ASD need extra support in acquiring personal and self-help skills, and this can place increased demands on parents, who have to try to find the extra time and patience to assist and/or supervise. Parents may have to aid in toileting, bathing, dressing, brushing teeth, and other daily tasks for a longer period of time than they initially expected. We often take for granted that kids will learn to become independent in these areas without much special teaching on our part, but some children need steps broken down and reminders for longer than others.

Start with small steps so your child can be successful. Often "backward chaining" can be helpful. That is, you help your child with all the steps, except for the very last one. For example, you can help him get his legs in his pants, but then step back to let him pull them up himself the last few inches. Once he's mastered that, you can let him pull them up over his knees, and then up from his ankles, and then inserting his second foot in a leg, and so on, moving backward in the progression of actions.

And shop around to make getting dressed easy on your child: there are clothes with magnetic closures (so you don't have to worry about those pesky buttons), slip-on or Velcro shoes (so laces can be avoided), and elastic-waisted pants (so zippers aren't a concern).

With toilet training, find a program (a simple search online should lead you to many recommended ones) that's quick and efficient. We've had good luck with the ones that include giving your child plenty of liquids to drink, so there's ample practice. Underwear and sheets with built-in alarms can be helpful in reminding a busy child to go to the toilet at the first drop of wetness.

As always, coordinate any independent self-help goals across settings. You want anyone who's spending time with your child to remind them to make regular stops at the toilet or, if relevant, to provide opportunities for them to take steps to dress independently. Progress is always fastest when there's consistency in the support.

Learn to Recognize Love, However It May Show Itself

Since some kids on the autism spectrum are sensitive to sensory input, they may feel overwhelmed by too much touching and may not seek out hugs, bedtime snuggling, or lap cuddles. And of course, a language delay may mean that the words "I love you" are a long time coming. If this is true for your child, you may find some comfort in learning to recognize their maybe less traditional signs of love in all of their wonderfully varied and myriad forms.

Maybe your child takes you by the hand and leads you over to something they've just made: that's love. Maybe your child seeks you out when they need something: that's love. Maybe your child lets you join them in their usually solitary play: that's love. Maybe your child doesn't hug you but always wants to be within a few feet of you: that's love.

You know that other people sometimes fail to see your child's intelligence because it doesn't always fall into the obvious patterns society expects. Similarly, your child's love for you may be untraditional, surprising, slightly hidden, but there if you know how to look for it. In chapter 3, "Communication: The Bridge That Connects," we suggest goals that will help round out your child's ability to tell you what they're thinking. Keep remembering that it was a hard task for your child to learn first words and requests. Now we're asking for some really abstract concepts, and many children need these to be taught and practiced.

Social Support

Most individuals diagnosed with ASD who are verbal report that they're eager for long-term friendships and romantic relationships. But differences with communication, nonverbal cues, and social anxiety may make it challenging to connect to people even when they want to. As a result, many young people on the autism spectrum may feel frustrated—and some may eventually give up trying for those meaningful connections, because they're just not coming easily enough.

As we've discussed previously, families of children with ASD sometimes choose to withdraw from social interactions and obligations, since it frees them from feeling judged and like they don't fit in. But the truth is we all need emotional support, and staying home may mean that parents and siblings lose out on the interactions and conversations that naturally occur during playdates, parties, and other social events.

It isn't fair that society makes it so difficult for autistic children to participate in leisure activities, and it's understandable if you've pulled back from signing your child up for after-school activities or going to class-wide get-togethers. Let's see if we can get that going again in a way that's comfortable for everyone.

So How Do You Get Out There?

Presuming competence and searching for those areas where your child excels (e.g., music, memory, art, visual abilities, organization, etc.) will guide you and your team toward landing on ways your child can find pleasure in being out in the world. Your child has strengths, and it's important to continually think deeply about those. Are there activities where those strengths can come into play? If, for example, your child loves to be on the computer, there may be a coding class that allows them to be part of a group, while also providing you with a chance to connect to the other parents dropping off or waiting for their kids.

Some children who don't enjoy sports may enjoy scorekeeping or simply supporting their team by cheering on good plays, which is fun and can easily be taught.

One boy we worked with loved repetitive actions. His parents bought him a yo-yo for his birthday, and he took to it instantly. He quickly became proficient at it, and eventually the school started a yo-yo club. He was by far the best in his class, which put him in the position of being able to offer advice and teach his peers new tricks. This helped him connect from a place of strength.

It may take some time and effort, but if you can find activities that your child genuinely enjoys and maybe even excels at, run by staff and leaders who are open to diversity, you and your child can both bene-fit. Your child will spend more time out in the world, learning to en-joy socializing, showing off their strengths, expanding and growing. And you'll be with parents whose kids have similar interests to yours and whom you can talk about adult stuff with. Win-win.

More Good News

The very good news is that parents of children with ASD report a lot of positives in their lives. Having an autistic child can bring exceptional and distinctive gifts to a family and a community.

DEEPER MEANING AND PERSPECTIVE

We all want our lives to have meaning, to feel like we're doing something more with our days than just getting through the hours, and parents of children on the autism spectrum often report an increase in that positive feeling. They find such satisfaction in the sense that what they're doing matters that they frequently pivot to careers and paths that allow them to offer autism-related support to others.

Quite a few of our parents have found ways to assist other families, advising them about transitions, IEPs, stress reducers, activities, and accommodations. No one knows as much as someone with personal experience, and sharing what you've learned with others who could use your advice is an excellent way to feel like what you do matters. (By the way, the desire to help others isn't confined to parents. We've had autistic students who decided to go into the field and are now actively helping others have a better life. And we've seen plenty of siblings show up at the table as well.)

A beneficial side effect of focusing on the big picture and helping others is that it usually reduces your attention to petty problems. Small worries often fade away, no longer worthy of concern. Parents who embrace the autism community report gaining perspective and focus and an ability to distinguish between what truly matters and what doesn't. Spilled drinks, burned toast, and other minor inconveniences just don't have much significance when you're spending your time fighting for people you love.

Many families discover that having an autistic child leads them to look at life with a more open and positive attitude than they had before. They may find greater pleasure in hearing their child use a pronoun correctly or get dressed independently than they ever expected they would. Simply seeing their child successfully interacting with a peer—something a parent of a non-autistic child might take for granted—can bring enormous delight.

Parents of autistic children take very little for granted; instead, they are grateful for every triumph, no matter how small, and that can increase their overall sense of positivity.

PERSONAL GROWTH AND MATURITY

Many parents report that their experiences in having a child on the autism spectrum have brought them increased maturity, as well as more sensitivity to issues of diversity and special needs. Having a child whose brilliance is often hidden teaches you to give other people time and space to show you who they are: you are less likely to judge other people at first glance, and that will increase your social circle and open your mind.

LEARNING THE UNEXPECTED

As we've discussed throughout this book, many children on the autism spectrum have intense interests, and their family members often decide to learn as much as they can about those interests, so they can share them. It's not surprising then that a lot of families report that their exploration into these various areas unexpectedly opens up whole new worlds for them. What may have started as a way to share something with a child or sibling sometimes turns into the acquisition of and delight in new and exciting ventures. We've known parents who have built on these passions and have even ended up actively engaging in or teaching subjects as far-ranging and fascinating as ancient history, flags, coins, bats, and outer space.

And all these journeys started with a child's initial fascination with something the families might never have thought or known much about otherwise. There is power and beauty in letting your child lead you places you never thought you'd go.

INCREASED EMOTIONAL CONNECTION

Many parents report that their family has forged a tighter bond as a direct result of having a child with ASD.

We mentioned earlier that some parents struggle with their child's social relatedness and difficulties expressing empathy, but, happily, despite these increased challenges, closeness doesn't seem to be an issue. Parents feel very close to their autistic child and feel happiness and fulfillment in their presence and in the relationship.

Similarly, despite an elevated risk of divorce, the families that *do* stick together report feeling closer than ever. They list greater partner satisfaction, an increased desire to plan for a future together, and a newfound respect for family members, many of whom have started contributing in new and unexpected ways. In short, they appreciate the cooperation and community that rise directly out of the unexpected journey of having a child with different needs.

EXPANDED SOCIAL NETWORKS

While it can be true that having a child with ASD makes certain kinds of socializing more challenging (and, again, we blame societal judgment for a lot of that discomfort), the truth is that it can also lead to new relationships that have the potential to be even more meaningful and rewarding than old friendships that may have become stressful. Many parents report that they've become close to other parents of autistic children, and that their child's support staff have started to feel like friends and family as well. There can be a built-in sense of connection in getting to know other people who are also aware of the importance of diversity and of embracing the unexpected triumphs and joys of having a child with differences.

INTENSITY

What all of the above shows us, if anything, is that life is lived a bit more intensely when you have a neurodiverse child. The highs are higher, and the lows can be lower. We want to help parents hold on to the highs—the closeness, the profound interests, the sense that their lives have meaning, the joy in small victories—while helping to defuse and tamp down the stress and isolation that too many parents are still reporting.

We have said repeatedly, and will continue to say, that if society welcomed diversity in all its myriad forms, a ton of stress on parents would instantly be eliminated. So we will continue to shout that from the rooftops and push for change.

Since that's a work in progress, though, what can parents do right away to help reduce their stress at home and out in the world, so they have the strength and energy to focus on their unexpected and wondrous life with their uniquely brilliant child?

Self-Care

Scheduling, organizing, arranging, and monitoring your child's support and school situation can be time consuming, and that's not even taking into account any other children in the family, who of course also need your care and attention.

One frustrating thing about stress is that it feeds on itself: feeling overwhelmed can cause focus and energy issues, and those, in turn, can lead to feeling even more overwhelmed and underwater.

There's no easy fix for this. In our opinion, a parent's psychological well-being isn't addressed adequately (and sometimes not at all) in teacher training programs, specialist training, or in society in general. There are no well-accepted guidelines for how best to support parents of autistic children, or for how to help them focus on and nurture their child's strengths—all of which would lead to an increase in happiness levels.

But while there may not be a concerted approach to reducing parents' stress, we do know some steps that have been proven to help.

It's important to note that these suggestions are not one-size-fits-all—the strategy that reduces stress in one person might inadvertently raise it in another. (Simply ask people what they think of meditation, and you'll see what we mean: it's a lifesaver for some, and torture for others.) So please reflect on which techniques help you feel better: if a strategy isn't working for you, drop it and try another. You'll know when you've found one that works for you.

One quick note: You may be tempted to turn to alcohol or drugs when you feel frazzled, and we get it. We've been known to have a glass of wine or two at the end of a long and difficult day. But do remember that overdoing alcohol and/or recreational drugs can actually make parenting more difficult, leading to a dangerous and escalating cycle. So avoid falling into that trap.

Try the following instead.

TAKE BREAKS

And don't feel guilty about it. Parents *need* date nights, alone time, and get-togethers with other adults, no kids allowed. We probably don't have to explain why this might help, but we would like to emphasize how important it is to make time for the occasional break, even if it seems challenging. It benefits everyone in the family. Our research has shown that parents who have a weekly date night report more satisfaction with the marriage and less stress overall.

Of course, it can be expensive to hire a babysitter, and if your child has delays in communication or unique behaviors, you may worry that a babysitter you *can* afford won't be knowledgeable enough to watch your child.

At our university clinic, we put together a list of college students who have an interest in autism and want to babysit. We share their contact information with parents looking for babysitting help. We urge other centers and universities to create their own lists; it may be worth checking with a clinic near you to see if that already exists, or maybe ask someone on staff if they know of anyone who might like to work some extra hours. You can also contact a psychology or special education professor and ask them to help you find interested students.

You may also want to try reaching out to friends and family for babysitting help. One couple we worked with arranged for their children to stay with an aunt once a month so they could have some time to themselves. They reported feeling completely refreshed after that monthly weekend break. (No information on how the aunt felt, but since she continued to offer the option, we assume she loved the time she had with her extended family.)

Regular exercise, yoga, and mindfulness training can all be welcome stress-relievers, and you might find a regular hourlong session easier to schedule than a whole night out or a weekend away. (See below for more on the importance of physical activity.)

Please don't convince yourself that it's more important to always be with your kid(s) than to take care of yourself. The truth is that feeling relaxed and in touch with your own needs makes you a better parent for them—and a happier human overall.

JOIN SUPPORT GROUPS

Some parents find support groups helpful. From the feedback we've received, parents want to make the most of this time (not surprisingly, since time away from the kids often requires expensive babysitting or begging a favor from a relative), and therefore prefer a support group that has specific, useful topics, such as how to write clear and measurable IEP goals, navigate successful family outings, decrease interfering behaviors, and so on. If you're interested in joining a group, you might want to check whether the one you're looking at is focused like that or has a more relaxed, "let's just hang together" kind of vibe—and, of course, if you prefer the latter for yourself, that's great, too. Sometimes sitting and chatting with people who get what you're going through can be just what you need.

EXERCISE

The research is unequivocal that physical exercise is good for everyone. Our own research shows that vigorous physical activity helps to improve academic performance, reduce meltdowns, and decrease interfering repetitive behaviors in children. Some parents also report that exercise helps their child sleep better. But children on the autism spectrum are often excluded from team sports and games, while busy parents often struggle to find time to exercise, despite copious research that physical activity can reduce depression and stress.

Given all the benefits, we recommend spending some time figuring out how to fit exercise for the whole family into your daily routine.

Some examples from our clinic: one family started riding bikes to school with their child, whenever time and the weather permitted; another found a way to spend an hour at their local pool several times a week; one mom routinely dropped her son and husband off several blocks from the house whenever they returned home after running errands, so they could have a short walk together.

Including regular exercise in your routine will help you feel better, think more clearly, and reduce stress. Plus, it can be a fun and enjoyable activity for parents and kids to do together.

SUMMARY

Tell yourself (and remember to listen!) that you're a good parent, doing the best you can for your child, with the knowledge and abilities you have at the current moment. Focus on the unique gifts your child brings to the world and figure out how you can help those gifts blossom and be recognized. Work collaboratively with the people you trust, and seek out people you can talk to and get support from. Find time for self-care and also for socializing with the people you love. If there's an activity you enjoy, try to find time to do it—you deserve relaxation and pleasure.

And ask yourself (and others if you want):

- *Are some of the wealthiest people in the world reporting that they're on the autism spectrum? (Yes.)*

- *Are some of our most famous celebrities open about being on the spectrum? (Yes.)*

- *Are most professors on the autism spectrum? (Yeah, probably.)*

- *Was Albert Einstein on the autism spectrum? (Most likely.)*

The list goes on and on and on. These people have used their gifts and strengths to improve the world, and your child can, too—maybe a little and maybe a lot. Anyone who interacts with autistic people knows what incredible strengths and gifts they bring to the table. Nurturing their talents can lead to great things for them, for your family, and for the world.

You're a parent, but you're also a person. The better you feel about the job you're doing as a parent, the happier you'll feel as a person. And happier parents have more energy and focus.

Now *that's* a cycle worth starting.

Acknowledgments

Many thanks to Karen Rinaldi and Kirby Sandmeyer for shepherding this project with enthusiasm and creativity. Alexis Hurley is responsible for finding this book a happy home, as she has been for so many of our projects.

And a huge thank you to Dr. Robert Koegel, Dr. Brittany Koegel, and Lizzie Ponder for reading earlier drafts of this book and providing feedback.

Index

About the Authors

DR. LYNN KERN KOEGEL and CLAIRE LAZEBNIK are the authors of *Overcoming Autism: Finding the Answers, Strategies, and Hope That Can Transform a Child's Life*, and *Growing Up on the Spectrum: A Guide to Life, Love, and Learning for Teens and Young Adults with Autism and Asperger's*.

Dr. Koegel is a clinical professor at the Stanford University School of Medicine in Stanford, California. She and her husband are the cofounders of the Koegel Autism Center at the University of California, Santa Barbara. She is the author of more than one hundred published scientific articles, the editor of the *Journal of Autism and Developmental Disorders* (JADD), and the author or editor of nine other books. She lives in Palo Alto, California.

LaZebnik is the author of ten novels, including *Epic Fail, Things I Should Have Known*, and *Knitting Under the Influence*. Her writing has appeared in numerous magazines and periodicals, including *Vogue*, the *Wall Street Journal*, and the *New York Times*, and in the anthology play *Motherhood Out Loud*. She lives in Pacific Palisades, California. Both authors have close relatives diagnosed with autism.